To my daughters' Granny and PaPa
(who happen to be my Mom and Dad)

JUST ONE OF ME

confessions of a less-than-perfect single parent

Dandi Daley Knorr

Harold Shaw Publishers
Wheaton, Illinois

Printed in the United States of America.

ISBN 0-87788-446-3

Library of Congress Cataloging-in-Publication Data

Knorr, Dandi Daley.
Just one of me : confessions of a less-than-perfect single parent / Dandi Daley Knorr.
p. cm.
Bibliography: p.
ISBN 0-87788-446-3
1. Single parents—United States. 2. Single parents—United States—Humor. I. Title.
HQ759.915.K66 1989
306.8'56—dc19 88-37310
CIP

---

98 97 96 95 94 93 92 91 90 89

10 9 8 7 6 5 4 3 2 1

Psalm 127

Unless the Lord builds the house,
  its builders labor in vain.
Unless the Lord watches over the city,
  the watchmen stand guard in vain.
In vain you rise early,
  and stay up late,
toiling for food to eat—
  for he grants sleep to those he loves.

Sons are a heritage from the Lord;
  children a reward from him.
Like arrows in the hands of a warrior,
  are sons born in one's youth.
Blessed is the man
  whose quiver is full of them.
They will not be put to shame,
  when they contend with their
    enemies in the gate.

Contents

Introduction

Okay, let's see what kind of parent you are. If there's no hope for you, maybe it's not too late to get your money back on this book. (But with your luck, you've spilled coffee on it, your kids have colored in the "o's," and your dog ate three pages.)

Quiz

1. The children have been snowbound with you for three days. You just *knew* they'd go back to school today—until you heard the 7 A.M. weather person announce: "No school today."

   Do you:

   a. Jump up and down, shouting, "Goodie! More time to spend with my darlings!"
   b. Try not to let the children see you cry?
   c. Send them off to school anyway?

2. When you take out the ironing board and iron, your child says:

   a. "Thank you, Mother (Father) dear, for ironing my sheets and underwear."
   b. "What is that thing?"
   c. "Please don't hit me!"

3. How many buttons are missing from your children's coats?

a. None. I have reinforced all buttons on coats, shirts, shoes, socks, toys, etc.
b. 37.
c. "Now, where are those coats?"

4. When your child seems to be coming down with a cold on a school morning, do you:

a. Keep him home just in case and serve *homemade* chicken noodle soup?
b. Take him to the doctor, then forget to give the medicine two out of the four times a day?
c. Apply make-up so his teacher won't notice he's sick?

5. When you vacuum:

a. Do you sing hymns and whistle while you work?
b. Do your kids run out and ask who's coming over?
c. You don't vacuum. (Go on to the next question.)

6. When—make that *if*—you had two free hours, would you rather:

a. Play trucks or Barbies on the livingroom floor or drive your kids to softball practice, ballet lessons, and the mall?
b. Clean under your child's bed?
c. Fly one-way to Tahiti?

7. Your family at the dinner table resembles:

a. Lifestyles of the rich and famous.
b. The Cleavers at the table, minus Ward.
c. The City Zoo at feeding time.

d. What table?
e. What dinner?

8. The neighborhood children know you as:

a. The mom with the kool-aid pitcher and chocolate chip cookies.
b. The Wicked Witch of the West End.
c. They didn't know your children had a mother.

If you answered *a* to all the questions above, put down this book immediately. Your problems are too severe to be dealt with in these humble pages. But if your answers were a smattering of *b's* and *c's*, read on—you may be a normal member of the human race!

I am in the middle of my single-parent struggle. As I write, I contend with Katy, my five-year-old, and her pressing demand that I join her for her favorite morning cartoon. How could I possibly prefer scribbling alone at my desk to watching ponies fly?

Last night I used up valuable work time listening to my seven-year-old lawyer, Jenny, present her case: "Thirteen reasons why kids should be allowed to stay up as late as mothers on Friday nights."

When a new acquaintance first suggested I write a book for single parents, I smiled politely and responded, "Spend forty-eight hours in my house and then say that."

"What are you talking about?" countered my new friend. "I've seen your kids—they're great! You've survived a rough divorce, your faith has grown—you're making it! Besides, wouldn't you love to read a book by someone who doesn't know it all, someone who doesn't feel like she has all the answers?"

Well, that's me. I certainly don't have all the answers. But I went ahead with the project, commandeering the help of hundreds of other single parents and their children. The children interviewed ranged in ages from two to fifty-two. (I can't tell you the ages of the parents; I had too much discretion to ask them.) I am infinitely indebted to these families who took the time to share their lives and wisdom on paper through the written surveys.

If it's true that only the ignorant live trouble-free lives, then we single parents must be among the wisest of people. I hope you find these pages practical. I know you'll find them real.

Dandi Knorr

PART I

THIS LIFE WAS NOT INTENDED TO BE
THE PLACE OF OUR PERFECTION,
BUT THE PREPARATION FOR IT.

Richard Baxter,
a Puritan forefather

AW, MOM, NOBODY'S PERFECT—
NOT EVEN PARENTS.

Jenny Knorr,
age seven-and-a-half

1

SUPERPARENT SYNDROME

Look! Up in the sky!
It's a bird—it's a plane—
it's Superparent!

THE FIRST TIME I MISSED MY daughter's Open House at school because I had a business meeting, I cried. I felt I had become one of *those* mothers. I had joined the ranks of mothers who couldn't be counted on to help out with the Valentine's Day party, carpool for soccer games, or sponsor a Brownies troop.

It isn't easy being a single parent. We're so busy changing hats (Mom, Dad, Breadwinner, Housekeeper, Playmate, Warden ...) that we don't get much time to stand in front of the mirror and take a good look at ourselves. Our reflections blur as we run past. There just aren't many quiet moments for objective meditation, so most of us aren't quite sure how we're doing in the single-parent role.

In today's hectic world, it's hard to keep a good perspective on ourselves as parents. When life moves along smoothly, we rarely notice those unobtrusive calms. When we run headlong into problems, we tend to focus on our mistakes and judge ourselves severely.

But—surprise! You and your kids are probably okay. Most likely you are a better parent than you think. The next few chapters of this book will help you find out.

Pressurized Parents

The pressure on us to raise bright children has never been greater than it is today. The result? We've become a new breed of parental hypochondriacs. We continually ask ourselves where we went wrong. We wonder, *What's the matter with my kids—and why?*

If your child isn't in a learning preschool by age three, how will he ever catch up? Billy and Amanda next door have had hands-on exposure to computers at their care centers since they were infants; your son still sleeps with his blankie. Your sister's kid knew all about Letter People by the time she was four; your four-year-old daughter can't even color and stay within the lines.

You thought you'd done great by reading to Susie since she was one—until you observed your pregnant coworker reading to her unborn child during coffee break.

You bought Jeffrey an expensive electronic learning toy for Christmas, but all he wants to do is watch the Rambo video his uncle sent him. Where did you go wrong?

Missy, your first-grader, is in the middle reading group, *not* with higher-track readers. And she brought home mostly *S's* on her report card. You're not sure what *S* stands for, but *E's* are better; and Marge's kids get all *E's*. What is Marge doing that you're not?

Greg is in middle school. All your friends with sons complain that girls call the house night and day for *their* boys. You think your son is handsome. Why don't girls call him?

Diane, your teenager, has turned on you. You can't believe this sassy creature is really your daughter. Now she tells you she doesn't even want to go to Disneyland with the rest of the family this summer! And she threatens to go live with Dad if you don't let her go to a three-day slumber party. Where did you go wrong?

The Trap Is Laid

Being a parent is a tremendous responsibility—one of the biggest jobs God assigns. We *should* take it seriously and work at becoming better parents. But we're not perfect—and God is not surprised. Kids are not perfect—and we should not be surprised. Our society has laid a giant parent trap for us. Consider a few underlying assumptions:

> Parents need to make their children develop intellectually as early as possible.
>
> The more advanced a child is in relation to his peers, the better off the child is.
>
> The brighter the child (higher achiever, better student), the better the parent.
>
> If something is wrong with the child, it must be the parent's fault.

As with most effective traps, the Superparent Syndrome contains some elements of truth. Children should be given a healthy environment to grow and develop. But how important is it for a child to be able to read before he is taught to read at school? Can we be sure that a child is well balanced developmentally just because he or she is advanced academically? And a child's problems don't necessarily reflect his home environment. Teenage delinquents come from unhappy, uncaring homes and also from solid, loving, Christian homes. Kids are people, too—with their own wills and their own imperfections.

Parents who fall into the Superparent Syndrome rarely enjoy their children—or allow their children to enjoy themselves. Each day is a preparation, a chance to push ahead toward the future, rather than a day to enjoy. "Parent Burnout" keeps cropping up as a hot topic in magazines. Why? Parents who try to be perfect and to make their children perfect may finally run out of steam.

After working on the research for this book for a month, I grew depressed. I despaired of writing a single positive word on the subject of parenting. The standards I'd read were impossible dreams. One book said that a mother should hold her baby every waking moment. A good mother creates a challenging, stimulating environment for her infant by decorating the baby's room in bright colors, hanging interesting objects from the ceiling, and playing classical music all night long. Well, my children are past nursery age; it was too late for me to do all those things.

Then I read some more—about parental appointments with children, the need for family councils, and the need for consistency. One mother said she sat in a rocking chair and knitted at least three nights a week so that her children would grow up with the same image of her that she'd had of her own mother. I sighed; I can't knit worth beans.

Sizing Up the Trap

So, how does a parent escape the pervasive Superparent Syndrome? Begin by sizing up the trap. Simply recognize that certain attitudes and vague guilt feelings lurk in every corner.

Knowing the trap exists is the beginning of your escape route. You can't dismantle society's system, but you can change your response to it.

Step two is to examine the conscious or unconscious measuring stick you're using to evaluate your effectiveness as a parent. From what sources have you picked up your standards of perfection? Most measuring standards fall into one of three categories: the *visible* parent, the *visible* child, or the *invisible* grandparent.

The visible parent

One day I took my daughter on a stroll to the park, where I overheard three moms discussing an absent mutual acquaintance.

"Emily is not a *visibly good parent*," remarked one of the mothers.

After various other moms were discussed, the final evaluation came down to the question of whether or not they themselves were "visibly good parents." One fortunate woman named Liz distinguished herself as visibly good. She was seen in the library with her children, taking advantage of the public story hour. She was frequently sighted in all the best playgrounds, encouraging her children to use the most creative play structures available. She attended public lectures on child-rearing and community improvement.

I waited until they left the park before I slinked over to the swings and reclaimed my environmentally underprivileged daughter. I hadn't known the public library offered a story hour.

Parents whose goal is to be "visibly good" may show up in all the right places. But does that mean they really are good parents? Their reasoning might sound something like this: *If I don't go to PTA tonight, everyone will think I'm not interested in my child's welfare*. Or, *My kids don't want to sit with me during church. What will people think?* And, *I'll bet everyone's wondering why I didn't sign up to help out with the school fair.*

The visible parent has placed his measuring stick in the hands of other people.

The visible child

"You're a wonderful mother. Your children are so polite and well-behaved!"

What mother wouldn't want to hear these words? Who wouldn't be willing to accept praise for her children's behavior? But the flipside of that golden coin of praise is that we parents must also accept responsibility for our children's poor behavior.

If you've ever dreaded those parent-teacher conferences, you understand the concept of *guilt by association.* You pace outside the classroom, waiting to see the teacher. As you approach the teacher's desk, you feel as if you're nine years old again and your mind scrambles to remember your best excuses. Maybe your hands shake and your knees knock.

In one of the books I read on single parenting, the author firmly applied the visible child measuring stick to test parent effectiveness. The opening chapter was entitled, "Parents Get the Kind of Kids They Deserve."

Parents slipping into the Visible Child Trap can be heard whispering to their children in public places: "At least try to act like human beings while we're here." Or, "Please don't embarrass me in front of my friends this time!" Or, "How could you do this to me!" And, "How many times do I have to tell you? If you want to throw food at each other, do it at home!"

These parents might be saying to themselves: *I don't know what's the matter with these kids. Where did I go wrong? What did I do to deserve this kind of treatment?*

The invisible grandparent

"If I had talked to my mother the way you talk to me, young man, she would have thrown me out of the house."

"When I was your age, my father made me mow the yard, plow the field, paint the barn, slop the hogs, and mend fences before I got so much as a nickel of spending money."

How many times have you heard or said something like that? The charm of the invisible grandparent measuring stick lies in the ease with which we can selectively remember how perfect we were when we were children. Of course we never got in trouble with the school principal or wiggled restlessly in church. It's easy to use this warped measuring stick to size up our own children.

Unfortunately, if we use this warped stick for our kids, we must also apply it to ourselves as parents. Logically, if we were such great kids, our parents must have done a much better job than we are doing. What parent wants to admit that?

What measuring stick do you use to determine if you are inadequate as a parent? Try to identify your phantom Superparent. Then face the phantom. Don't stand next to your dream-parent and feel belittled. It won't do you or your children any good.

The Great Escape

After you've taken a long look at your version of a superparent, you need to look in another direction. Take a long look at God—he gave you your children. He's not surprised at the job you're doing with them. If he felt you couldn't bring up those priceless human lives—his creations, his children—he could have arranged for someone else to do the job. He knows you better than others know you, even better than you know yourself.

Let God be the one you run to for conviction, for approval, and for help in parenting. Other people can offer valuable advice. Listen to it, but filter it through Christ. As the bumper stickers and refrigerator magnets say, *God isn't finished with you yet.* No one is born a good parent. Consider 1 Corinthians 1:26: "Brothers, think of what you were when you were called. Not many of you were wise by human standards; not many were influential; not many were of noble birth."

It's better for you and better for your kids if you answer to the Lord and not to public opinion about your skills as a parent.

Watch out for the Superparent Syndrome! God is the only Superparent.

Things to Think About/Discuss

1. Describe in detail your vision of the superparent.

2. When do you feel most guilty about your shortcomings as a parent?

3. Did anything happen recently which made you feel inadequate as a parent? Jot down some notes about the event or attitude. How valid was your self-doubt?

4. Do you feel any pressure to be a "visibly good parent"? How might you begin to dismantle that trap?

5. How do people view your "visible child"? How have positive and negative comments affected the way you feel about yourself as a parent?

6. Describe the "invisible grandparent" in your home. Can you identify any guilt or pressure you have placed on your children or yourself because of this phantom?

2

THE SINGLE-PARENT TRAP

SINGLE PARENTS FACE THE SAME parent trap other parents face, but single parents are exposed to another, even more dangerous, trap. The following excerpts from my old journals provide clues to what it is.

Diary of a Trapped Single Parent

> Katy's nearly two and still can't talk, except to say "da da"—of all things! I don't spend enough time with her. I don't talk with her enough—not as much as I did when Jenny was a baby. When I had a husband to help me, I was free to be a better mother.
>
> Jenny's in bed and crying to stay up. Should I go to her again? She's already had water, three kisses, two hugs, another bedtime story, a potty attempt, a bandaid on one finger, and the

nightlight lit. But what kind of mother lets her daughter cry herself to sleep? If I were a better parent, Jenny would be asleep by now. There's only me to consult here. How can I know if I'm too lenient or too strict when I don't have another parent around to give me perspective?

How can I be so mean? I have the sweetest kids in the whole world, and I yelled at them! They deserve two great parents, not one crummy one.

I'm so ashamed. My one thought all day has been, "I can't wait until their bedtime." I live for eight o'clock! Wouldn't it be wonderful to have a husband who could help with dinner and baths? We'd all go out for a family stroll or bike ride after dinner. But instead I'm so tired, I can't even stroll upstairs to tuck the kids in bed.

Jenny's teacher asked me if something was the matter at home. Jenny has been acting sad at school. When Mrs.—asked Jenny, Jenny said she missed her dad. I'm such a lousy mother! First, my daughter isn't happy with me but wants to be with her dad. Then she doesn't even tell me she is sad and misses him!

Today I saw a young couple with a little girl at the park. Both parents played their hearts out with that kid. All three rode the merry-go-round and went down the slide. Mom and Dad smiled at each other, sharing their delight in their child. I spent most of my time running between Katy and Jenny, each of them feeling slighted and sincerely believing I paid more attention to the other one. How can I be both father and mother? I'm not two people!

Gosh, my kids are lousy eaters! It must be because I settle for easy meals now. If we were a regular family, I'd have enough energy to fix real meals, and their father would make them eat!

How I hate to discipline the girls! Just once I'd like the luxury of saying, "Just wait till your father gets home!"

The Blame Game

When we single parents have problems, our single status provides a convenient scapegoat. There are many variations to the blame game. We attribute our problems to our divorces, our ex-spouses, our loneliness, or any one of the creative labels that stem from the fact that we're parenting alone.

Adopted children have a similar temptation. When adopted children go through the traumas of adolescence, they experience the emotions all teens do: they feel different, out-of-place, as if they don't belong. But adopted teenagers have a ready scapegoat to explain their difficulties. They can point to their problems and blame the fact of their adoption.

Single parents may do the same thing with their singleness, appealing to the fact of their aloneness to explain every parenting problem.

Martyrs

Single parents make wonderful martyrs, and sometimes it's hard to resist the temptation and ensuing comforts of martyrdom. We feel we're doing our best, but it's an impossible situation. One parent just can't do the work of two. No matter what our teenagers think, we simply can't drive in two directions at once!

One parent candidly told me: "A number of things are actually better for us (her daughter and herself) since my divorce. But I hate to admit that we're happy." It's so hard to let go of that martyr image!

I am the first to admit the truths inherent in the single-parent trap. Single parenting *is* a tough assignment. Single parents have lost the system of checks and balances, of division of labor. There's no other parent around to monitor how we deal with our children day in and day out. No one points out the inconsistencies in discipline or the blocked perspective on a single issue or offense. The burden of our children's problems falls on our shoulders, and it's a heavier load when it's not divided with another parent.

But you can triumph. You *can* debunk the scapegoat and dismantle the single-parent trap. It may make you feel better to blame your problems on your singleness, but it seldom helps you discover solutions. In fact, martyrs usually reproduce little martyrs, who use their status as "deprived children" to get away with murder.

Scapegoats

Let's take an honest look at the scapegoat of singleness.

We would have many of these same problems even if we weren't single parents.

Within six months after my divorce, I ran into a large deer on a snowy highway, lightning struck a tree in front of my home and sent the tree crashing onto the hood of my parked car, a bat made his home in my attic, I was sideswiped by a hit-and-run driver, both of my daughters had to have their tonsils out, our landlord decided to sell our rental home, and I was audited by the IRS.

I felt like a true martyr. But I can't say conclusively that those traumas and tragedies would not have befallen me if I had still been married.

Regular families have problems, too.
The problems which seem to derive from our single-parent status can often be found in stable, loving, two-parent families. Well-adjusted fathers and mothers receive plaintiff calls from their children's teachers. "P.K.'s" are notoriously naughty, so obviously all preacher's kids are not trouble-free. No parent is immune to the potential dangers of the teenage years, when a young person begins to look to his peer group structure instead of Mom and Dad.

Some two-parent homes function as single-parent families.
This is surprisingly common. One parent may assume sole responsibility for the children. One may become the caretaker, the chauffeur, the responsible party, to the exclusion of the other parent.

Most of my fantasies about being a happy homemaker with time for my children, time to take up knitting, and time to keep a spotless home, are unrealistic. I was surprised to discover that fewer than 20 percent of American families consist of a father who works and a mother who stays home full-time to spend time with her children. And even in those families who plan on sharing parenting, it's easy for a workaholic dad or mom to drop out of the parenting picture and let the other spouse function as Dad *and* Mom.

There may even be some advantages that accompany the single-parent life.
One parent may provide a healthier environment than two parents who are constantly engaged in heated battle or locked in a cold war. The children of a single parent might miss the close-up view

of a healthy, happy marriage, but they may also escape a negative, distorted view of what their parents' marriage was like.

Being the only parent around may even make it easier to develop deeper relationships with your children. Parent and child share more experiences and responsibilities and usually play a larger role in each other's lives. *Parents Without Partners* is a national association of single parents, with local chapters all over the country. In one PWP study, nearly all single parents found that their parent-child relationships had improved since the end of their marriages.

Logistically, a single parent may discover parts of herself/himself that were swallowed up during marriage.

As a single, you may have more time to curl up by the fireplace with a good book on Sunday afternoons instead of watching ballgames. Now you may take up golf again, without feeling guilty for leaving a "golf widow."

Please don't misunderstand. I'm not advocating the choice of being a single parent. I believe God's plan includes mother, father, and children living happily ever after. But for some of us, Plan A is no longer an option. And we're not doomed! We *can* have healthier, happier single-parent families than we had as two-parent families. A single-parent family can work and work well.

A friend of mine, also a single mom, related to me how her fifth-grade daughter came home from school one day, threw down her books, and complained, "Why can't we be a normal family?"

My friend braced herself for the inevitable onslaught of comparisons between her own deprived daughter and her daughter's more fortunate friends who still had a mother and a father living with them. "A normal family?" my friend ventured.

"Yes," said her daughter. "Where the kids see their dad every other weekend, and the parents don't hate each other just because they're divorced." My friend and her daughter had different standards for *normal.*

What is a normal family? What is a desirable home? There are good and bad single-parent families and good and bad two-parent ones. Let's steer clear of the single-parent trap we set for ourselves, and let God make us the best parents we can be—even if we're less than perfect.

Things to Think About/Discuss

1. Describe the ideal single parent.

2. Describe your own single-parent trap. Begin, "If I weren't a single parent ..."

3. Complete this sentence: "I feel the heaviest weight of responsibility as a single parent when..."

4. Respond to each of the following statements. Is the statement true, partially true, or false?

a. Parents need to make their children develop intellectually as early as possible.
b. The more advanced a child is in relation to his peers, the better.
c. The better a child is, the better the parent is.
d. If something is wrong with the child, it's the parent's fault.

5. How do your answers to the statements above reflect your view of yourself as a parent?

3

YOU'RE IN MIGHTY GOOD COMPANY

I MAY HAVE BEEN THE FIRST SINGLE parent in my family, even the first single parent among my friends, but I am *not* the first single parent in the history of the world. Don't feel alone—you're in good company.

The Discarded Wife

Hagar was Sarai's Egyptian maidservant. God had promised Sarai's husband, Abram, a multitude of descendants who would become a great nation, the people of God.

But Abram wasn't getting any younger, and neither was Sarai. She was past the normal childbearing years. So she came up with an idea to help God fulfill his promise (as if God needed her help!). She gave her maid, Hagar, to her husband to get a child by proxy.

Abram consented, and Hagar became pregnant. But Sarai, feeling jealous, resented her maidservant and mistreated her. And that's how Hagar became the discarded wife.

While still pregnant, Hagar set out on her own and ran away to the desert. But the angel of the Lord met her there. He spoke of Hagar's unborn son, Ishmael, and declared, "The Lord has heard your affliction." God had watched over and heard this single mother, but her problems were not over.

Hagar agreed to return to Sarai and Abram. Hagar gave birth and remained in Sarai's household until her son was a teenager. But on the day Isaac, Sarai's and Abram's natural son and miracle baby, was weaned, Hagar and Ishmael were sent off into the desert.

Mother and son wandered through the desert until, completely out of water, they sat down to cry and wait for death. Hagar put her only son under a bush and moved away, saying, "I cannot watch the boy die."

What happened next is encouragement for any single mother who has ever been distressed over her child:

> God heard the boy crying; and the angel of God called to Hagar from heaven and said to her, "What is the matter, Hagar? Do not be afraid; God has heard the boy crying as he lies there. Lift the boy up and take him by the hand, for I will make him into a great nation."
>
> Then God opened her eyes and she saw a well of water. So she went and filled the skin with water and gave the boy a drink.
>
> God was with the boy as he grew up. He lived in the desert and became an archer. *Genesis 21:17-20*

Have you ever felt discarded and alone against the world? The next time you're despairing, remember Hagar and God's shout from heaven: "What's the matter with you, Hagar? I heard the boy crying!"

God hears our children, our teenagers. He knows where they are and what they need, even when we don't. God takes a personal interest in our families and wants to protect us.

God had to open Hagar's eyes before she saw the well he had provided. Once God opened her eyes, Hagar got up and gave her son a drink. If we're too busy crying over our children's deprivations, we may not see God's provision of resources.

Finally, the Bible says that God was with Ishmael as he grew up. They didn't move back into the luxurious, six-bedroom, three-bath tent; Ishmael had to grow up in a desert. But there in the desert, Ishmael became an archer, probably a better archer than he would have become in his old environment.

God uses our circumstances to mold our children into everything he created them to be. We have a choice. We can stand off a few paces and complain about being thrown into the desert, where our children don't seem to have as many advantages as other children and where we feel deprived of former comforts and luxuries. Or we can open our eyes to discover what God has in store for our children. We can let God lead us to the well, where we'll find exactly what our children need.

Daddy's Boy All on His Own

By the time Joseph was seventeen, his mother had died and he had incurred the hatred of his brothers for being Jacob's favorite son. Joseph's brothers sold him into slavery to a band of Ishmaelites (descendants of Hagar's son) who took young Joseph to Egypt. Joseph went from living the life of a daddy's boy to enduring the life of a slave.

In Egypt, Joseph, with no parental guidance, rose from slavery to great power. He became ruler of Egypt, second only to Pharaoh. In this pagan environment, he worked hard, resisted sexual temptations, forgave his brothers, and exemplified generosity toward men and trust in God. All this he did without Mom or Dad!

Joseph could have ruined his life by using his miserable circumstances as an excuse: *Why me? Why did I lose my mother? Why was I torn from my father, uprooted from my old life?* But Joseph opened his eyes to the God of his family, his God, and Joseph turned out great!

God won't necessarily keep bad things from happening to our kids. Joseph spent years in jail! But God was in the jail with Joseph. "But while Joseph was there in the prison, the Lord was with him; he showed him kindness and granted him favor in the eyes of the prison warden" (Genesis 39:21). There's no place our kids can go, no trouble they can get into, that God won't be there with them.

Miracle Man

Moses' mother gave up her three-month-old baby in order to save his life. He was raised by a substitute single mom, Pharaoh's daughter. Moses made mistakes, faltered, but triumphed with the faith of his parents and trust in God.

The Bible comments, "Since then, no prophet has risen in Israel like Moses, whom the Lord knew face to face, who did all those miraculous signs and wonders the Lord sent him to do in Egypt—to Pharaoh and to all his officials and to his whole land. For no one has ever shown the mighty power or performed the awesome deeds that Moses did in the sight of all Israel" (Deuteronomy 34:10-12).

Many of us can't give our children as much time as we'd like. We've had to use daycare centers, nurseries, babysitters. It's reassuring to know that we can still have a great deal of influence on our children. Moses lived among non-believers and was exposed to a lifestyle far removed from that of his parental home. Yet he grew up with their strong values and living faith.

The Visiting Parent

Once upon a time, there was a woman named Hannah. She wanted to be a mother desperately, so God gave her a son, Samuel. When Sam was three years old, Hannah gave up custody rights. Sam was placed in a foster home, under the care of a man named Eli. It was decided that Hannah would maintain reasonable and seasonable visitation. Once a year she visited her son and brought him a present.

So Samuel grew up without the continual presence of his parents. But the Bible tells us: "The boy Samuel grew up in the presence of the Lord" (1 Samuel 2:21).

In the same temple household lived Eli's two sons, Hophni and Phinehas, making an early blended family. Although they were priests like their father, Hophni and Phinehas were disrespectful, ungodly, and immoral. Samuel, instead of being raised in Hannah's godly family, was exposed to the corrupt living of Eli's sons.

Hannah believed she had done the best thing for all parties concerned. Indeed, she had even started another family. Yet she worried about Sam. Sure, Eli was a good man, but those sons of his! They were not the sort of kids she wanted her son to have for friends. She had heard all kinds of stories about those boys. But what could she do?

Because Hannah was a Christian, she prayed fervently for her son. She knew God could be with Sam, even when she could not. And when she did have visitation, she made the most of her time with her son.

When Sam was of age, he began to visit his mother more often. And he grew into a fair, honest, godly man. Hannah was very proud of him.

If you can only see your children under limited visitation, and you fear your influence can't stand up to their new environment, read 1 Samuel for encouragement. Samuel turned out great! He listened to God and ruled as a judge over Israel all the days of his life. We don't have all the details on Samuel's further contacts with his family, but the last verses in 1 Samuel 7 suggest his strong ties to his home.

> From year to year he went on a circuit from Bethel to Gilgal to Mizpah, judging Israel in all those places. *But he always went back to Ramanah, where his home was,* and there he also judged Israel. And he built an altar there to the Lord. *1 Samuel 7:15-17, emphasis mine.*

The Kid King

Josiah was eight years old when he became king of Judah. His father, Amon, had been assassinated in his own palace by his own officials. Amon had been an evil king, much worse than Josiah's grandfather, Manasseh.

Now Josiah, with the help of his mother, began his thirty-one-year rule in Jerusalem. Josiah had dreadful examples to follow in Amon and Manasseh. Logically, Josiah should have become a wicked king. But Josiah did what was right in the sight of God. God himself called Josiah humble and tender-hearted.

When Josiah was sixteen, he began to seek God. Four years later, he began to reform Judah and Jerusalem. He destroyed idols and repaired the temple.

During the work on the temple, the book of the law given to Moses was discovered. Josiah read the Law to the people and made a covenant to keep the Word of the Lord.

When Josiah died, the record in 2 Kings 23:25 said of him:

> Neither before nor after Josiah was there a king like him who turned to the Lord as he did—with all his heart and with all his soul and with all his strength, in accordance with all the Law of Moses.

Most of us single parents would be more than satisfied if our children earned such a tribute at the end of their days. Did Josiah do better without a father? We can't say for sure, but it's doubtful Amon would have approved or allowed his son's reforms. Whether you believe it or not, your child's environment, with all its shortcomings, may be the best one for him.

The Good Widow

It must have been an awful day when Naomi's husband, Elimelech, died, leaving his widow with two sons to raise in a foreign country (Moab—where the family had been forced to flee during a famine). Then about ten years later, Naomi's sons, now married to Moabites, also died. Naomi experienced the stress we would expect from someone who has lost husband and sons and is left in a foreign country alone. "It is more bitter for me than for you," she told her daughters-in-law, "because the Lord's hand has gone out against me" (Ruth 1:13b). "Don't call me Naomi (*pleasant*)," she told them. "Call me Mara *(bitter)*, because I went away full, but the Lord has brought me back empty. Why do you call me Naomi? The Lord has afflicted me; the Almighty has brought misfortune upon me" (Ruth 1:20-21).

But Naomi didn't focus on her own dilemma for long. She looked past herself and realized the plight of her daughters-in-law, who would be left childless and without husbands. Naomi encouraged them to remarry—not an easy choice for a mother-in-law, who would be left without support. One daughter-in-law accepted Naomi's offer and returned to her own people. But Ruth chose to stay with Naomi.

The result? God took care of Naomi and Ruth. At the end of the story, Ruth is remarried, and Naomi holds Ruth's baby boy in her lap. The neighbor women declare, "Naomi has a son" (Ruth 4:17). And that child became the father of Jesse, the father of King David, the forefather of our Lord Jesus.

Widows and Orphans

God provided for care to be given to widows and orphans. He promised to be a father to the fatherless, and to protect widows and orphans. "Do not take advantage of a widow or an orphan," God declared to Moses in the Law (Exodus 22:22).

Elijah and Elisha performed miracles to rescue single-parent families. Elijah met the widow at Zarephath just as she was preparing what she believed would be the last meal for herself and her son. At Elijah's instruction, the widow first fixed a small cake for Elijah. Miraculously, the Lord provided for her little family; the bowl of flour and jar of oil remained full for many days.

Later, when the woman's son grew sick and stopped breathing, Elijah prayed to God and restored the boy to his mother.

Elisha, Elijah's successor, rescued a widow whose creditor threatened to take away her two children as his slaves. Elisha effected a miracle, enabling the widow to have oil to sell and pay her debt, with enough left over for her family to live comfortably.

Jesus showed a similar concern for widows and their children. He praised the widow who put only two coins—all she had—in the offering. He felt compassion for the widow of Nain, whose only son had died, and he raised the boy to life again and gave him back to his mother. He condemned the Pharisees for devouring widow's houses.

James even defined pure religion in the sight of God as "to look after orphans and widows in their distress and to keep oneself from being polluted by the world" (James 1:27).

You Mean I Didn't Blow It?

What can we learn from the examples of early single-parent families? When we think about Joseph or Moses or Samuel, we can stop feeling sorry for ourselves or our children. Our children can reach their full potential in every way: spiritually, intellectually, emotionally, vocationally, and professionally.

God has a plan for our children—the same plan he had when he formed them in the womb. We haven't destroyed their chances for fulfilling that plan.

God isn't surprised that our children are part of single-parent families. He doesn't stomp his foot and say, "Rats! Now what can I do with those poor kids? That parent really blew it!" God could raise our children all by himself if he wanted to. But he has chosen us to help.

I could sketch colorful scenarios of successful single-parent families I've met over the past three years. Some of the best parents I know just happen to be single. You are in mighty good company.

Things to Think About/Discuss

1. Have you ever felt alone in the challenges of single parenting? What circumstances made you feel that way?

2. Have you ever felt "discarded" like Hagar? Is there anything in Hagar and Ishmael's story to give you hope?

3. Ishmael became a great archer when he was confined to the desert. Have you noticed any positive developments in your children which might be a result of living in your single-parent home?

4. Of the singles touched on in this chapter, with which biblical character do you identify most? Why?

4

GOD THE FATHER

The summer I lived in inner-city Los Angeles, I was a happily married woman. I attended a church with a high percentage of single-parent families. In that church, I heard some of the best singing in the world. Each Sunday, as they marched down the aisle, the choir sang,

> Praise the Lord,
> For he has been so good to me.
> He's been my father, my mother,
> Sister and brother.
> For he has been so good to me.

I had no idea how important those words would become for me about five years later as a single parent. Because then I began to understand God as the one who could fill every earthly role: father, mother, sister, brother, husband, wife, friend.

Is Anybody Listening?

When I asked Jenny's kindergarten classmates, "What does God look like?" I was in for a surprise. The kids knew—or at least they thought they knew.

One little boy's description of God was quite detailed: "God has *big* hands, a huge head, gigantic eyes, a *humongous* nose. But his ears—they're as little as mine."

Who hasn't felt that way? When the kids are fighting, when someone else got the job you applied for, when the bills refuse to pay themselves, and you haven't met an interesting man/woman since 1983, you start to wonder if anyone is listening when you pray.

Even King David, who affirmed his faith saying, "I waited patiently for the LORD; he turned to me and heard my cry" (Psalm 40:1), had moments when he felt God couldn't possibly be listening.

Hear my prayer, O LORD,
  listen to my cry for help;
  be not deaf to my weeping.
For I dwell with you as an alien,
  a stranger, as all my fathers were.
Look away from me, that I may rejoice again. *Psalm 39:12-13*

Listen to my prayer, O God,
  do not ignore my plea;
  hear me and answer me.
My thoughts trouble me and I am distraught. *Psalm 55:1-2*

I am worn out from groaning;
all night long I flood my bed with weeping
and drench my couch with tears.
My eyes grow weak with sorrow. *Psalm 6:6-7*

God hears us—all the time. There's nowhere we can run where we will be out of earshot. What does this mean to me as a single parent? It means I am never really alone. There is always God, the Father who hears.

Does Anybody Care?

But God does more than just hear; he listens and cares. God lets me pour out my heart to him and cry on his shoulder. I can vent my anger to God—instead of taking it out on the children. I can talk to God about financial worries, instead of complaining to my oldest daughter and adding stress to her life. God is always attentive.

We have a compassionate Father. "Just as a father has compassion on his children, so the Lord has compassion on those who fear him" (Psalm 103:13).

Jesus wept for Martha and Mary when they lost their brother. He stood on the hill overlooking Jerusalem and cried for the city that refused to be comforted. God promises to wipe all our tears away one day. Through Isaiah, God promises, "As a mother comforts her child, so will I comfort you" (63:13).

Because I care deeply for my children, I wait to hear the accounts of their days. If Katy is happy because she got to be helper at preschool, I'm happy too. If Jenny is sad because one of her friends didn't want to play with her at recess, I fight back my own tears. I want to know everything about my children! And when the only response I can get out of them after school is, "I don't know," or "I don't remember," I feel left out.

God waits for us to discuss our days with him. He cares with perfect, parental love.

Sit Still!

I had looked forward to Katy's second birthday more than Katy did. Carefully I had selected the most lovable doll she couldn't destroy in ten seconds and a handsome stuffed puppy of exact size and shape to render it impossible to insert in her mouth.

The night before her birthday, I stayed awake wrapping, fussing, dreaming.

When Katy awoke, she caught my excitement. She darted from room to room and danced in circles. At last she opened her present from Jenny, a toy pony. She jumped around with it for an hour, introducing it to the other toys. I couldn't get her to come back to the table for her other presents—the ones I wanted to give her.

Finally, I carried Katy, kicking and screaming, to the table, forced her to sit down, and made her open her presents. What an exhausting experience! I love to give good gifts to my children, but they have to sit still long enough to receive them.

"If you, then, though you are evil, know how to give good gifts to your children," said Jesus to his followers, "how much more will your heavenly Father give good gifts to those who ask him!" (Matthew 7:11).

God waits to give us good gifts, to take care of us as our perfect Father, but it's hard to present a gift to a moving target. Psalm 46:10 says, "Be still, and know that I am God." We need to slow down and take time to see the gifts God has for us.

The Father Who Disciplines

God is the Father who hears and the Father who cares; he is also the Father who disciplines. We inherit a legacy of blessings from our heavenly Father, but those special attentions naturally include fatherly discipline.

Every parent fights the battle of toy pick-up. My daughter Jenny knew she was responsible for keeping her toys picked up, even when she had a friend over to play. One Saturday, Jenny and her friend Sarah got out every toy they could find. The house looked as if the ceiling had rained toys.

"Jennifer Anne Knorr!" I called in my sternest mother-voice. "Get this stuff picked up, and get it picked up now!"

Seeing little Sarah hiding behind Jen, I said in a much gentler voice, "Would you mind helping her, Sarah?"

Then turning back to Jenny, I raised my voice: "Get going, and don't throw anything under your bed. Put them away!"

As I started to leave the room, I heard Sarah ask Jenny, "How come your mom's meaner to you than she is to me?"

I strained to overhear Jenny's response: "Oh, that's nothing. She yells more at me 'cause I'm her kid. She cares more about me growing up messy."

We may feel that as God's children we should have an easier life. But if anything, because we are his we should expect more suffering, more discipline.

In Philippians Paul expressed his desire to know the fellowship of Christ's suffering (3:10). James said we should rejoice when we encounter various trials (James 1:2). God cares for us. He doesn't want us to grow up messy.

God is our Father. Picture Jesus on the hill, overlooking your family. He wants to gather you as a hen longs to gather her chicks. Let him. Let him be your Father.

Things to Think About/Discuss

1. Name three things you have admired or appreciated about your own father. Can you see those traits in God?

2. Think of one fear, one insecurity, or one secret you don't want anyone to know about. Talk it over with God right now. Remember—he is the hearing Father.

3. How has God shown his compassion for you in the past month? Be specific.

4. Do you find it hard to "sit still"? What can you do to insure a few quiet moments in your day to meet with God?

5

GOD THE HUSBAND/PARTNER

A father to the fatherless, a defender of widows,
is God in his holy dwelling.
God sets the lonely in families.
Psalm 68:5-6

THE AWESOME RESPONSIBILITIES of single parenting struck me from an unusual angle the last night of summer vacation. The following is an excerpt from my journal.

> If I wanted to I could send Jenny to school in a formal gown and a pair of my high heels. Or, I could make her go in a swimsuit. I could decide to keep Katy home from preschool. I could lock her in her room until she turns twenty-one (at which point I would lock her in her closet). I could pack up all our stuff and move us to Iceland or Tunisia. I could get a snake for a pet, or fourteen turtles, or both. It's all up to me.

Many single parents share my sense of awe at being solely responsible for other lives, the lives of their children. Here are some of the fears other single parents have expressed. Although most of the comments were made by custodial parents, non-custodial parents admitted similar fears.

> I try hard everyday, but I'm afraid I can't fulfill all my children's needs.
>
> The worst thing about being a single parent is the awesome responsibility. Talk about a heavy burden!
>
> It's too easy to make a wrong decision when there's only me.
>
> I feel my aloneness the most when I have to make a decision.
>
> I can't be the male *and* the female role model!
>
> The stress of being totally responsible almost makes me collapse and give up at times! This undermines my efforts to give steady discipline, and it negates some of the good things going on in our family.
>
> The kids have only me to count on—in an emergency, or in everyday routines.
>
> The hardest part is the *total* responsibility.

The visitation parent may also feel a frustrated sense of responsibility.

> I want to be a good example for my daughter. How can I do that with only four days a month?
>
> I'm supposed to be there to help her through her day-to-day problems. But she lives four hundred miles away.

There are so many things I want to pack into the weekend I spend with my boys. I only get two days to be a good father.

Such a heavy responsibility is almost enough to make a single parent cry out for help. You need a partner—someone to share the load, help with decisions, talk things over with!

Let's Advertise

Female (male) person, once reasonably sane, attractive, and fun, seeks individual meeting the following qualifications. He (she) must:

1. *always be there for me.*
2. *be a good listener*
3. *be faithful and trustworthy.*
4. *always be thoughtful.*
5. *be patient and forgiving.*
6. *be exceedingly wise, good at decision-making.*
7. *love children.*
8. *love me.*
9. *like me.*
10. *make allowances for the fact that I do not meet the requirements above.*

While you're wishing for Mr. or Ms. Right, consider God's offer. If God says he is the father of your children, that also makes him your life-partner.

Our Life-Partner

Let's examine how God meets all the requirements of our Mr./Ms. Right advertisement.

God is always there.

Even if you were happily married, your partner couldn't *always* be around when you needed him or her. God can. "God is our refuge and strength, an ever-present help in trouble" (Psalm 46:1).

There is no place you can go where God isn't. When you're caught in traffic and feel like throwing your shoe at the guy who just cut in front of you, God is there to calm you down. When it's forty minutes past curfew and your teenager still isn't home, God is there; you don't have to wait alone. When your sixteen-year-old announces his plans to drop out of school because he wants to make money *now*, God hears that, too.

The possibility of intimacy lies with God. He knows all your ways; nothing is hidden from him. He offers his secrets to those who love him. He desires truth in your innermost being. And when you let your guard down, when you tell God the worst about yourself, he isn't shocked. He knows already! And you never have to regret your words. He's closest to you when things are at their worst. As Psalm 34:18 says, "The Lord is close to the broken-hearted."

God is a good listener.

Since God is always present, he hears everything, and he understands every word. "Pour out your hearts to him" (Psalm 62:8).

When there's no child support check *again*, you can voice your complaint to God (*before* the kids come home from school and you have to tell them: no check, no Pizza Hut).

God listens, even when we're not talking. He knows our thoughts even before we speak them. When we get up in the morning, God is there to talk over the scheduled events for the day. "Praise be to the Lord, to God our Savior, who *daily* bears our burdens" (Psalm 68:19).

God can listen to any problem on-the-spot. Then at night, he's ready to help us take off our burdens so we can get a good night's sleep.

God is faithful and trustworthy.

If we didn't know from personal experience that God is faithful and trustworthy, we know it's true because the Bible says so: "And the faithfulness of the Lord endures forever" (Psalm 117:2). And, "The one who calls you is faithful" (1 Thessalonians 5:24).

Some single parents have gone through experiences that make it hard to trust another person again. Faithfulness is becoming a lost resource.

But we can trust God. He doesn't lie, and he won't change his mind about loving us. We don't need to guard ourselves or our hearts against God. We can safely put ourselves in his hands.

Other single parents may have been unfaithful themselves while they were married. Now they suspect God may not be faithful to them. But God promises that even when we are faithless, he remains faithful.

We *can* trust God. He won't desert us, give up on us, or change toward us. He is faithful and trustworthy.

God is thoughtful.

The Bible also teaches us that God thinks about us. Psalm 139:17-18 says, "How precious to me are your thoughts, O God! How vast is the sum of them! Were I to count them, they would outnumber the grains of sand."

These are some of the nicest words: "I thought about you all day." Doesn't it make you feel wonderful, important, and loved when you know someone is thinking about you?

One of my first dates was with a guy who lived in a small town thirteen miles from my home. I don't remember many details of that date, but I do remember the fifteen minutes before my date rang my doorbell. I stayed in the bathroom, brushing my hair, putting on lipstick, and practicing smiles. But I was consumed with the idea that Jeff was already on the road, heading for my house. He had to be thinking about me. He was driving fifteen minutes—for me. I was in his thoughts, for fifteen minutes at least.

Even the slightest acts of thoughtfulness can earn deep impressions. About the only thing I remember about John, another boy from my young dating years, was his habit of shielding me from inclement weather. If it looked like rain, John had an umbrella for me. If we were out and the weather turned cool, John would give me his jacket. Even while driving, John would unconsciously adjust the sun visor on the passenger side of the car to keep the sun from hitting my eyes.

And of course I'll never forget the fellow who sent me flowers the day the St. Louis Cardinals lost the World Series.

It colors our thoughts about ourselves to know we are in the thoughts of someone else. And you know what? God is constantly thinking about you.

God is patient and forgiving.

In an impatient world that expects more from us than we are able to produce, where people demand us to be finished products rather than people-in-progress, where forgiveness rubs against the grain of human self-love, it's wonderful to have a Partner who is patient and forgiving.

Scripture is full of praise for God's patience and forgiveness: "For his anger lasts only a moment, but his favor lasts a lifetime" (Psalm 30:5). Exodus 34:6-7 reminds us: "The LORD, the LORD, the compassionate and gracious God, slow to anger, abounding in love and faithfulness, maintaining love to thousands, and forgiving wickedness, rebellion and sin." In the New Testament, Peter encourages us with these words: "The Lord is not slow in keeping his promise, as some understand slowness. He is patient with you" (2 Peter 3:9).

God won't storm out of the house in a fit of rage. He won't threaten to leave if we make the same mistakes over and over. He isn't waiting for us to blow it again so he can yell at us or throw things. God patiently waits for us to learn from our mistakes.

God also forgives. He won't throw those mistakes back in our faces later. He chooses to forget, to give us a fresh start every day, if we need it. (And who doesn't?)

God is exceedingly wise.

Having another adult to help make decisions in the family should strengthen the decision-making process, but two heads do not guarantee a wiser solution to the problem.

An unwise person simply wouldn't be much help. One divorced woman commented, "The best thing about being a single parent is that I don't have to suffer because of ——'s crazy ideas. I can make sane decisions for my family without damaging interference."

But with God it's different. There's no fear that God will steer us wrong. There are times when I wish it were easier to discern his advice on *specific* issues like: Where should I send Katy for therapy? Should I apply to teach at a small college? Should we move to a different house?

But as our relationship with Christ deepens and we learn to communicate with God in prayer and in Bible study, discerning his will becomes easier. May this be our prayer: "Teach me to do your will, for you are my God; may your good Spirit lead me on level ground" (Psalm 143:10).

God loves kids.

"I'm sorry. I like you, but I've already raised children. I don't think I'm interested in going through that again. Goodbye." Does this sound familiar? Or, "Oh, I didn't realize you had the kids this weekend. Maybe next weekend would work out better. Bye."

Maybe you just found the man/woman of your dreams: attractive, wise, intelligent, and trustworthy. But if your prospective partner doesn't love kids—*your* kids in particular—your relationship is doomed.

Recently a survey was given to people who had tried and failed with a second marriage where kids were involved. Participants were asked to give the main reason for the marriage breakdown. Three-quarters of those asked gave problems with the other guy's kids as their reason.

But God loves your kids more than you do! Your children are already God's children—there's no adjustment involved.

God loves me.

God's love is complete—and unconditional. It doesn't matter how we act or look. He loves us without make-up. He loves us when we get up in the morning, before we shower and shave. He loves us when we're not lovable to anyone else.

In Romans, Paul argues that Christ's death proves God's love for us (5:6-8). Someone might be found to die for a good and righteous person, he argues, but Christ died for us while we were still sinners.

A Hebrew word, *hesed*, used in the Old Testament for God's unique love, has no direct English translation. Our Bibles use various words or phrases to try to communicate that quality of love expressed in *hesed*: lovingkindness, mercy, everlasting love, compassion, covenant love. *Hesed* is a love that lasts because it does not rest on the object of love, but on the giver of love, God.

God likes me.

We need people who love us, and we need people who like us. Do you have any relatives you love, but you really don't like? You love Aunt Agnes, but she's the last one you'd want to take with you on a vacation. You're fond of your neighbor, but he's really not your type.

One morning when I woke up feeling odious to everybody (even the cat hid from me), I happened across these verses:

> The LORD your God is with you,
> he is mighty to save.
> He will take great delight in you.
> He will quiet you with his love,
> He will rejoice over you with singing. *Zephaniah 3:17*

God says he will take great delight in me. I need to have someone feel that way about me! I delight in my daughters; I smile inside with incomparable pride when I look at them. I love to watch Katy swing in the backyard, or see Jenny come skipping down the sidewalk after a long day at school. Nothing gives me more pleasure than to see those girls happy, enjoying themselves, and discovering the world around them.

God delights in me like that, and rejoices over me with singing.

God makes allowances.

Our previous advertisement for a Partner presents an extensive list of qualifications. I certainly hope no one will ever expect *me* to fill that bill. God knows I can't live up to all those expectations. He knows me well enough to know what to expect from me. He makes allowances. My younger daughter, Katy, has a learning disability. If you don't know her and her capabilities, you can easily frustrate her by demanding of her something she is incapable of doing.

I'm the same way when it comes to machines. Don't talk to me about changing my computer menus and processing my data. And don't think that just because I can get a book into and out of my computer, I can balance my checkbook or file anything. But if your expectations are reasonable, you can expect me to be reasonable.

God is reasonable. "For he remembers that we are dust" (Psalm 103:14b). God created us, knows us better than we know ourselves, and has seen our every weakness. And he loves us anyway!

Tap into the Source

There may be another earthly partner for you just around the corner. But there may not be. In either case, take advantage of all that's offered to you in Christ.

Can God be a valid member of your single-parent home? The Book of Deuteronomy directs us to talk about God and his holiness with our children when we lie down, when we get up, and all during the day (6:6-9).

I'll never forget the natural response I got from a little first-grade boy when I asked a group of children, "Who is Jesus?" With no hesitation, the boy volunteered, "He's Mary and God's boy. I talked to him last night." Let Mary and God's Boy be an integral part of your home.

Things to Think About/Discuss

1. When are you most overwhelmed with the burden of responsibility for your family? What do you do about it?

2. In your opinion, what is the hardest part about raising children alone?

3. If you were going to marry again, what qualities would you look for in a spouse? List them in order of importance.

4. How does God measure up to your list of qualifications? Be specific.

5. What can you do to make your partnership with God more real to you?

PART II

CHILDREN TODAY ARE TYRANTS.
THEY CONTRADICT THEIR PARENTS,
GOBBLE THEIR FOOD,
AND TYRANNIZE THEIR TEACHERS.

Socrates (470-399 B.C.)

6

WHAT'S GREAT ABOUT ME?

IN MY ZEAL TO INSTILL CONFIDENCE in my children, I'm afraid I become a cheerleader. There I was, trying to compensate for Jenny's inability to cut on the lines as she chopped out dubious shapes from a piece of typing paper. "Wow, Jenny," I raved. "Those are wonderful! Those are just great."

Jenny fingered the paper pieces, tilted her head to one side, and looked up at me with a knowing grin. "Oh, Mom—these ones are great. These ones aren't."

What a gift—to see ourselves accurately and clearly—and to accept what we see! What a gift it would be to see our children accurately, clearly, and accept what we see. Happy, healthy children don't just happen. They usually spring from happy, healthy parents. Before we can talk about accepting our kids, we may need to work at accepting ourselves.

I believe most parents want to encourage their children and would like to be able to say, "Great!" But many of us single parents feel so overloaded, it's hard to see greatness in anything. If we have fallen into our single parenting by divorce, or if we suffer from continual guilt feelings that somehow we're not doing enough for our children, we may feel anything but great about ourselves. And if a parent is denying all greatness in herself, how can she acknowledge greatness in her child?

Strengths vs. Weaknesses

As parents, we need to see greatness in ourselves, to recognize our strengths and our successes. And we have to be mature enough to admit our weaknesses and learn from our failures.

Children have similar needs. When a child feels that nothing he does is good enough, he may stop trying. The toddler taking her first steps looks around for approval. The three-year-old rolling out of his first somersault waits for applause. Even the kid who's just learned to ride his bike isn't satisfied until someone sees him ride.

Every child needs to know there is something great about him. A parent is best qualified to point out greatness; parental approval carries the most weight.

But every child also needs to recognize his weaknesses without feeling defeated. In the next four chapters, we'll talk about handling strengths and weaknesses—our own, and those of our children.

Great Value

All of us have seeds of "great" in us because God made us in his image, and images reflect the original. A human being is an extraordinary work of art. Aside from anything you'll ever do, you are of immense value simply because you are a person, a creation.

Remember how Jesus reassured his disciples when they began to worry about what might become of them? He didn't point out all the wonderful things they had accomplished on earth. He didn't tell them, "Don't worry, you have helped so many people, done such good jobs with your ministries, that I'm sure God will take care of you."

Instead, Jesus called their attention to the birds of the air: "They do not sow or reap or store away in barns, and yet your heavenly Father feeds them. Are you not much more valuable than they?" (Matthew 6:26).

Even while we were at our worst, God considered us valuable enough for Christ to die for us (Romans 5:8). If you're having one of those days (or weeks or years) when you can't find one thing you can point to and say, "This is great," remember, *you're* still great. You're valuable because God loves you.

Great Gifts—Me?

Some of us have never thought of ourselves as great, or gifted and talented, in anything. Or, if we have suspected greatness, we have been quick to deny it.

How do you take a compliment? When someone says, "Boy, you look nice today," what do you say?

Oh, I do not.
No, I've had this coat for twenty years.
You're just saying that. You're the one who looks great.
Sure.

If someone comments on how well you play the piano, hit the baseball, or look after your children, which of the following is most likely to be your response?

Oh, you're just trying to make me feel better.
I was just lucky today.
No, I'm not really that good. You should see so-and-so! He's really good.

Is it so difficult to smile and say, "Thank you"—to accept a compliment? If it's hard for you to accept praise from others or to praise yourself, figure out why. In my talks with other single parents, I've come up with three possible explanations for resistance to acknowledging one's own gifts and greatness. I'm sure there may be many possible explanations; these are just the ones that kept cropping up in my discussions with other single parents: basic insecurities, lack of self-grace, and a misunderstanding of humility.

Basic insecurities

Basic insecurities can keep us from seeing any greatness in ourselves. One divorced mother of three told me, "I don't think I can do anything right. My husband said so; that's why he left me. My teenagers are convinced their mom is from another planet (and they'd love for me to return there as soon as possible). I'm scared to death that they'll fire me every time I mess up at work. And as far as getting married again is concerned—who would want to get stuck with me?"

This woman couldn't see herself as she really was: an attractive, professional woman who provided financially for her family, did a great job of raising three children by herself, and worked unselfishly in her community. Her mindset was framed to see herself as inadequate and incompetent. That perspective was her filter. She rejected every bit of conflicting information that might have shown up her areas of greatness. Her successes were consistently stifled by her insecurities.

If you feel as if you can't do anything right, you need a new filter, a new mindset. Try the mind of Christ, who sees you through the eyes of love. He delights in you and thinks you're great. He knows you make mistakes but sees you in the light of eternity, as you will be. See yourself as his treasure, his inheritance.

Check your focus. Is your vision so fixed on the last stupid thing you said or did that you can't see the good things going on in your life? You can choose your focus. You can't control which thoughts pop into your head, but you can choose how long you're going to go over and over those thoughts in your mind.

I still get renegade thoughts from something that happened five years ago: "Why did I do that? If only I would have said this and then done that differently ..." But I have the choice whether I want to spend the day criticizing myself or change mind channels and think of something else.

Philippians 4:8 reads, "If anything is excellent or praiseworthy, think about such things." The alternative (not found in Scripture, of course) would be: "If there is anything crummy, if anything worthy of getting down on yourself, let your mind dwell on these things."

Lack of self-grace

A lack of self-grace can keep us from feeling great about ourselves. "Why should I expect anything to turn out great after all the mistakes I've made? I made such a mess of my marriage, I don't deserve another chance."

It's hard for us to forgive ourselves. But sin is the great equalizer. We're all in the same courtroom; we all deserve death, according to the Scriptures:

> There is no one who does good, not even one. *Psalm 14:3b*
> For all have sinned and fall short of the glory of God. *Romans 3:23*

If you, O LORD, kept a record of sins,
O LORD, who could stand? *Psalm 130:3*

But God has showered us with his grace. Christ has earned forgiveness for us. So we can forgive ourselves. He sets us free to see good things, *great things*, in ourselves.

What do you say when someone expresses amazement that you're raising a family all by yourself? The person generally follows this with, "I could never handle the kids by myself. I have my hands full as it is. How do you do it?"

I usually decline the compliment: "Ha! Follow me home and spend the night. Are you kidding? You should have heard me yell at the kids in the car on the way over here. I almost rolled down the windows and forced them to jump!"

Accept God's grace to cover your mistakes, so that you can develop self-grace, or forgiveness, for yourself. There is no Perfect Parent Award. Don't let your lack of grace deny your "greats." We need all the grace and greats we can get.

Misunderstood Humility

Misunderstanding humility can keep a lot of great people from feeling great. Some of us believe we are being good people, good Christians, when we refuse to see anything positive in ourselves. True, the Bible says, "Humble yourselves, therefore, under God's mighty hand," but we need to be careful in our interpretation of humility. Paul warned the Colossians against delighting themselves in false humility (Colossians 2:18).

We shouldn't have to work at humility. We don't have to deny our greats to remain humble. Perfect humility means perceiving ourselves accurately, as we really are; it's having a correct evaluation of ourselves. If we refuse to admit our gifts, talents, and strengths, we will never see ourselves accurately.

Jesus used children to teach his disciples about humility. Once he surprised them by calling over a little child. He said, "Therefore, whoever humbles himself like this child is the greatest in the kingdom of heaven" (Matthew 18:4).

How do children humble themselves? It isn't by intentionally putting down their achievements. It's not through their conscious efforts to deny greatness. My younger daughter is just moving out of the stage where she thinks Mother knows best. Whenever Katy used to have a problem, she would come directly to me to make it okay. When a block wouldn't fit into a hole, she'd hand it over, confident I'd get the job done. If her hands were sticky, she'd stick them into my face so that I would see and remedy the situation. If she tore the arm off her baby doll, she'd come to me. The thought never entered her mind that I wouldn't know what to do.

But of all the times Katy brought some problem for me to set right, I can never remember her feeling bad about herself—until she got older. The fact that she couldn't get that puzzle piece in the right spot may have frustrated her sometimes, but it didn't make her give up. She knew what she could do, and she acknowledged what she couldn't do.

All of us have enough weaknesses and inabilities that we shouldn't feel we need to deny our abilities and strengths. To admit the *greats* doesn't mean you deny the *not greats*. You're just seeing yourself straight.

Go ahead and look for the things that are great in you. Someone who has suddenly become single through a death or divorce is usually forced to attempt new things. Many single parents discover, or rediscover, buried talents. One single dad commented, "I found out I'm a great cook, and I thought I couldn't warm beans."

A single mom shared, "For so many years I believed I couldn't do anything right. Now I'm managing a household and holding down a full-time job. I'm even reading the newspaper—front page *and* editorials!"

Give yourself some credit. If you are a single parent and still alive, you are amazing! Most of us are doing things we never dreamed we could do. We're more efficient because we have to be. We're tougher, because we have to be. We get back up when we're knocked down because we can't just lie there when the kids are depending on us. We're resourceful because it's the way to survive.

Ask God to reveal to you your gifts, your talents, your strengths. We all need the freedom to point and say, "These are great!"

Things to Think About/Discuss

1. What is there about the human body, inherent in every human being, that is "great"? List at least five specific wonders.

2. How do you normally respond to a compliment? List as many compliments paid to you by others as you can remember. How did you respond to each?

3. List five gifts or talents you possess, things that come easily or naturally for you.

4. Make a list of things you have done or accomplished in the last year that you used to think you never could do.

5. Name five things you are doing "right" as a parent.

7

ACCEPTING THE NOT-SO-GREATS

Every failure is a step to success;
every detection of what is false
directs us toward what is true.
William Whewell, English philosopher

Failure is often God's own tool
for carving some of the finest outlines
in the character of his children.
Thomas Hodgkin, English historian

EVERY LIFE HAS A FEW NOT greats. What do we do with our failures and weaknesses? I think we have three choices when we're faced with things that fall into the "not great" category: 1. We can wallow in our weakness; 2. we can deny the problem; or 3. we can accept and adjust our attitudes and actions.

Wallowing in Weakness

I have this game I play all by myself. It takes place inside my mind. Maybe you play it, too. I call it the *Square One Game*. As with most board games, there are spaces I move along on my journey, trying to reach the winning goal. *Successful mediation of an outbreak of sibling rivalry:* advance one square. *Lost two pounds:* advance two squares. *Sold an article to a major magazine:* go forward three squares.

But inevitably, I'll land on a "not great" or a "failure" square: *rejection of book outline by publisher*, or *no date—again!*, or *was reprimanded at work*, or *yelled at the kids*. If I land on one of the failure squares, I have to go back to Square One. It doesn't matter how far I've advanced on the board toward my goal, I still have to start all over again. All previous progress is discounted.

When we wallow in our weaknesses or failures, we lose perspective. Don't go back to Square One! One mistake doesn't make you a lousy mother or a terrible father. Weaknesses and problems in one area of your life don't disqualify you as a capable person.

Realize that a weakness may be a strength. Remember when Jesus described the Pharisee and the tax collector who were praying in the temple? The Pharisee, far from wallowing in his weakness, was expressing thanks that he had none! The tax collector, on the other hand, felt so burdened with his sin, he wouldn't even look up. The tax collector was bringing his burden to the right place. Jesus said it was the tax collector—not the Pharisee—whose prayer would be heard. In a way, his weakness became his strength.

Admit your weakness or failure or sin. But don't play the Square One Game. You don't have to start all over from the beginning. Christ has won our forgiveness. God's power is perfected in our weakness. When we are weak, he is strong. Toss that shortcoming, that mistake, to God and let him take care of it while you keep moving ahead. Change the rules: *You don't have to go back to Square One when you goof up.*

Denying the Problem

"It wasn't my fault."

"Don't blame me."

"This never would have happened if...(if they weren't out to get me, if he hadn't played up to the boss, if they hadn't provoked me in the first place, if people would leave me alone, if people would help me out)."

"The devil made me do it!"

I personally don't mind failure—unless it's mine. It's no fun to admit failures or weaknesses. During recovery from a crisis, denial can protect us emotionally until we're strong enough to deal with the realities. But prolonged denial can prove dangerous. Denial may make it easier, more comfortable for now, but it usually demands payment later.

Listen to this single mother:

> I'm just fine. Really, I'm doing great! I thought I'd be lonely because I don't have time for friendships, but I've discovered I don't need friends because I'm so happy being myself. Work? I know I'm doing a great job. Of course, I'm not one of the boss's pets, so I don't always get a raise when I deserve one. And the kids? They're great! They don't miss their father at all, and they are so happy in school.

If this single parent is trying to convince herself that her life is great, she may be able to carry it off for awhile. But what happens when she runs into something she can't deny? What does she do when her son is arrested for drunk driving? Blame the kids he hangs out with? What does she do when she can no longer convince herself that she is happy in isolation? When denial and reality finally meet, it'll be explosive!

People talk about a "positive self image." We're told to build ourselves up, to "self-talk" praise and admiration. We cherish the *Little Red Engine That Could* (and did) and tell ourselves that we're a breed of superpeople.

We expect ourselves to do it all—family, career, ministry. If we can't meet all those expectations, maybe we can pretend we *do* meet them. And if we say it often enough, we may even believe it. And if we believe all that positive self-talk, then maybe we'll really be great and have great self-esteem.

But what if we still aren't capable to do what we've been told we can do? What happens then? Please don't misunderstand. We need to have confidence, to focus on the positive, to give up self-defeating attitudes. But we can do this without sacrificing reality, without pretending.

Mature optimism, mature positive thinking, can't deny the present when it focuses on the future. The present is simply put into a better perspective.

Denial involves deceit, and deception is dangerous. The Scriptures warn us: "So, if you think you are standing firm, be careful that you don't fall" (1 Corinthians 10:12). And, "If we claim to be without sin, we deceive ourselves and the truth is not in us" (1 John 1:8). Psalm 32:2 challenges us: "How blessed is the man ... in whose spirit there is no deceit."

If we deny our "not great" areas, we won't take responsibility for our actions, and we won't grow up. We'll make the same mistakes and fail to recognize them as mistakes. A person who exits one marriage, insisting, "It's all his fault! I did everything I could to hold that marriage together, but he divorced me anyway. He's completely to blame!" is a good candidate for a second divorce.

I'm all for a healthy self-image. But an unrealistic, inflated view of self is not healthy. A healthy self-image sees accurately and understands that God isn't finished yet. Yes, God created us in his own image, but remember—he used dust.

Adjusting Actions and Attitudes

When you tread into your "not great" arenas, remember that you are more than the sum of your actions. Just because you *do* something dumb doesn't mean you *are* dumb. You don't have to return to Square One. You don't have to deceive yourself into believing what you did was really quite great. You can admit that it was not but know that God isn't finished with you yet.

God's economy of self-worth and greatness is different from the world's. God says the last shall be first, the greatest shall be the servant. "For he who is least among you all—he is the greatest" (Luke 9:48).

Things to Think About/Discuss

1. Do you tend to wallow in your weaknesses or deny them? Give specific examples.

2. What do you see as your most glaring weakness, the one that frequently makes you return to "Square One"? Next time you are tempted to go back to Square One, what can you do?

3. Describe your definition of a healthy self-image.

4. What is your biggest hindrance to accepting yourself? What can you do to begin to see yourself as God sees you and accept yourself as he does?

5. Take an honest look at yourself and analyze your strengths and weaknesses. Make a list with two columns, headed "strengths" and "weaknesses." Then pray and thank God for both lists. How can you tap into one strength this week? How can you begin to work on one weakness?

8

CHILD-SIZED GREATNESS

I called my mother and told her
I quit biting my fingernails.
She called me a quitter.
Anonymous

HOW CAN WE ENCOURAGE OUR children and make them feel great? I think we have to consider two major pieces in the parent's puzzle of acceptance. First, parents must be able to accept greatness in their children. Then they must convey their acceptance and affirmation to their children.

Gifted Parents = Gifted Kids, Right?

Emily put all her energies into raising her daughter. She knew Catherine had what it takes to succeed. Emily wanted the best for her daughter, everything she had never gotten out of life when she was young.

But Catherine had different ideas. With all the advantages she had been given, Catherine still wasn't succeeding. Emily paid for private dancing lessons for three years. Yet Catherine still hadn't distinguished herself; she just wasn't working hard enough at it.

Catherine gave up the piano; she never practiced anyway. And even though Emily did everything she could to spur Catherine on to higher grades, she still brought home *B's*. Emily didn't know what else to do with her daughter.

Ben had the same problem with his son Tim. Ben's other son, Dan, was great. Ben and Dan loved to fish and hunt together. And wow—could Dan hit a baseball! But Tim liked to read, and he played the flute. Ben couldn't see any hope for the kid.

Jan had always been an *A* student. She had just assumed her children would follow in her footsteps. They did not.

Perceiving Greatness

Probably each of us could compile a long list of "unacceptables" about our children, although we probably wouldn't admit that we don't *accept* them. After all, we clothe and feed them. Everything we do is for them. We love our kids! Who could say we're not accepting them? We just want them to be better than they are. Or we can't understand why they continually fall short of our expectations.

How can you know if you are accepting your children or if they feel accepted? Your child may send out warning signals that he fears he's not accepted. He may give up, just quit trying. Or he may become the perfect child and do everything he can to please you and earn your love. He may feign indifference or come out fighting. He may get into drugs, or end up with straight *A's* (and ulcers).

Know Your Child

Seven-year-old Jackie came home in tears. "I hate music!" she shouted.

"Jackie," said her mother quietly. "What's the matter? You love music."

"It's the music teacher at school," Jackie explained, trying to hold back the tears. "Every day he gets mad and yells, 'Sit up straight! Feet on the floor!' He never even sees that my feet can't reach the floor!"

If we don't know our children—see them as they are, listen to them—we will often make unreasonable demands of them. Before you can accept your child meaningfully, you may need to work on getting to know your child.

Julie brings home a *C* in math on her report card. How should you react? If you know that Julie is bright, likes math, has always gotten *A's* before, and that her teacher mentioned Julie's knack for figures, you probably would have a different reaction than if you knew Julie had worked her heart out for that *C* and couldn't be expected to earn a *B*. But if you don't really know Julie, how can you know what type of affirmation she needs?

Some parents naively pressure their children into becoming chips off the ol' block. It is terribly stressful and disappointing when the children don't share their parents' dreams and aspirations. These parents aren't acquainted with their children's dreams, with what *they* want to be and do when they grow up.

Paul wrote these words to the Colossians: "Fathers, do not embitter your children, or they will become discouraged" (3:21). Another translation says, "Do not *exasperate* your children." We exasperate our children when we expect behavior from them which they are not capable of producing.

Did anyone ever try to make you run faster than you could run? That's exasperation. Have you ever been asked to put together your child's costume for the play—by tomorrow night? That's exasperation. Did anyone ever expect you to be lovely, gracious, and charming, when you felt exhausted, hostile, and depressed? That's exasperation.

Exasperation is what your teenager feels when you expect him to think and react just like you. It's what your first-grader feels when you continually lose patience with his faltering attempts at reading. It's the way your fourth-grader feels when she's tried her best, but knows you'll be disappointed that she didn't make the soccer team.

Our children become exasperated when we have unreasonable expectations of them. How can we have reasonable expectations if we don't know them well enough to know what to expect? Knowing takes time, patience, and wisdom. It may mean letting go of our own dreams for our children so that we can hear their dreams for themselves. It may mean giving up the goal of making them everything *we* wanted to be. Our children are unique creations of an all-wise God—it may be an exciting surprise to watch their dreams unfold.

Getting to know your child is a life-long adventure. Children keep changing. Just because Peter wanted to be a doctor when he was three doesn't mean he won't decide to be a cowboy at five. You have to keep up on those things.

You don't need to know your child very well if you intend to use other children as the standard for evaluating your child's work. It's dangerous to measure Susie's progress against Heather's achievements. Maybe Heather is a musical prodigy and Susie's advancements at the piano will pale in comparison. If you want to encourage your child meaningfully, you need to know her well.

Your Child in Perspective

As you grow in the knowledge of your child, you will be better equipped to see him and what he does in a clearer perspective. You'll be able to recognize his greatness.

My younger daughter, Katy, has a learning disability that affects her speech. Her sister Jenny and I have come to recognize every consonant that is new or difficult for Katy. When Katy uses one of those sounds correctly, Jenny and I are ready with praise.

The Bible says that Mary noticed things about her son Jesus and treasured them in her heart. One of my biggest treasures is the memory of my daughters greeting each other in the back of the station wagon after I picked them up from school one Friday. Katy looked up with hopeful eyes at her sister and said, "I Katy." It was the first time I had ever heard her articulate "K" and "T" correctly, clearly pronouncing her own name.

Jenny grabbed her sister and gave her an enormous hug. "Oh, Katy, that was great! You said, 'Katy!' "

That was the best encouragement Katy could have received. Jenny *knew* Katy, and she had Katy's abilities and accomplishments in perspective.

If we're not careful to keep our children in their own, and in God's, perspective, we will miss their *greatness* when it comes along.

Present-tense Acceptance

Most children focus much more solidly on the present than we do. They haven't lived long enough to see the future become near reality. They need to believe that they are doing great *now*.

If all a child ever hears is that "one day" he will be like his big brother, or that "one day" she will be beautiful or talented, that child may become frustrated rather than encouraged. "One day" may seem too far off to help the way he feels today.

We want our children to know that they are great right now. Communicate your confidence that they will do great things, be great people in the future. But also communicate that right now, they're great kids.

Conveying Greatness to Your Kids

Bob's son Jeff was a great kid by just about anybody's standard. If there was an award at school, Jeff would likely win it. He played on the starting basketball team in high school, even though he was only a sophomore. And he was a nice, well-mannered, popular student.

Bob grew up during hard times. He had been forced to drop out of school after the eighth grade in order to help support his family. Bob had done well for himself and his family. He had worked two jobs while Jeff was growing up; now he had a well-paying, prestigious job at a large company.

But Bob didn't have much in common with Jeff. They didn't talk much. Bob was proud of his son, but Jeff had no idea of his father's approval. In fact, Jeff was certain his father disapproved of everything he did. Jeff had always supposed it was because he had chosen to be involved in sports at school—sports left him no time to work a part-time job after school. He assumed his father thought he was lazy and resented the time he spent on basketball.

Bob never attended Jeff's basketball games. Jeff figured it was because his father thought basketball was a waste of time. Jeff didn't know that his father basked in the afterglow of his son's victories. At the office, Bob let the guys know his son had been the star the night before. But Bob didn't go to his son's games because he was afraid Jeff would be ashamed of him. After all, Bob had never finished school. He knew his English wasn't first-rate. Sadly, Bob's and Jeff's lack of communication continued through adulthood.

Bob truly thought his son was great, but Jeff never *felt* his father's approval. Accepting our children may not help them if they aren't able to see and feel that acceptance.

How can we let them know we think they're great? Here's some of the best advice other single parents have given me regarding conveying acceptance. And gratefully I pass along their wisdom.

Catch them being good.

From the time our kids are small, we try to catch them being bad. One single mother reported that she tries to catch her kids being good. Building character is more easily accomplished when we can reinforce good behavior.

So look for desirable behavior in your children, and tell them about it on the spot: "Beth, you did such a good job putting on your own shoes without a reminder from me." "Jim, I admire the way you practice shooting hoops so faithfully every night. You never skip that practice time, even when the weather's awful." "Girls, I can't tell you how much I appreciated your lowering your voices while I was on the telephone."

We'll still have to handle the undesirable behavior, but it may be easier if we've been fair and noticed the positives along with the negatives.

Give 'em credit.

Another single parent made this point: "Give 'em credit. Even when you have to look and look, you can usually find something to give your kid credit for. You know you can always find something to blame him for."

At this very minute, as I am trying to type at my computer, Jenny sits at her little desk next to mine, supposedly making a flower picture. She has been home with chicken pox for eight long days.

In the past thirty minutes, Jenny has given me the history of the brontosaurus, considered the pros and cons of seven different colors of construction paper she might employ in her flowers, offered to type her name on my computer for me, and had me help her find her scissors.

A couple of minutes ago, I delivered an eloquent lecture about the importance of my work in my office, pointing out my generosity in allowing her to cross the threshold in the first place. If I choose to follow this single parent's advice to give Jenny credit, even though I don't feel like giving her credit, I could point to several things. It *has* been almost two minutes since she spoke. She *did* say she was sorry for disturbing me. It *is* creative to be making flowers out of construction paper. She *has* been a good sport about all those ugly, itchy pox spots all over her, and she *has* fought the urge to scratch. We've been trying to keep up on her homework, and it hasn't been easy. I never dreamed they did so much actual work in the first grade! I could tell her I admire how many different things she's learning, how much work she does every day, how quickly she seems to pick up math.

Or I can keep on typing and miss the chance to give her credit, to catch her at being good. It's up to me.

Don't hurt the ones you love in order to impress those you don't really like.

This advice came from a woman who realized she was hardest on her kids when they were with her co-workers. She was the only single parent on the floor where she worked, and she wanted the others to know her kids were great. She wanted to make sure they knew she was a good mother and handling home as well as work.

Every time they went out for hamburgers with her co-workers, she'd coach her children before they got there and criticize them after the meal. Then one day she wondered, "Why am I hurting the ones I love just to impress people I don't really care about?"

Your kids themselves are more important than the impression they make on others. They know when you're using them to impress your friends.

Compliment the right stuff.

"I try to focus my compliments on things over which my children have control," wrote one single parent. "What good does it do for me to reinforce constantly how gorgeous my daughter is? Now and then, such praise can make her feel good about herself. But isn't it better to point out that she's really good with her hair, that she seems to have a knack for fixing it? Wouldn't it be more helpful for me to tell her I think she did a good job coordinating her colors or staying on her diet?"

Compliment the right way.

Your child has just been chosen to represent his class in the city spelling be. Analyze the following possible responses and what each response might instill in your child.

> It's about time. You'd better get on the ball and study. Hundreds of kids and parents will be watching to see how you do.
>
> Finally that teacher of yours has used some sense and stopped picking her favorites for everything.
>
> You mean you beat out Sarah's son, Johnny? Way to go!

All right! I always knew you had more brains than any of those other kids. You'll knock 'em dead!

Spelling bee? I didn't even know they had those anymore.

Fine. You couldn't make the football team, but you're an ace speller.

Your work paid off. I'm so proud of you!

That's wonderful! Good spelling is a skill you'll use your whole life.

There are a lot of ways to give a compliment. Can you detect the mindset behind each compliment above? Children pick up a good deal of their perspectives from their parents: myopic and self-centered, competitive and vicious, defeatist or insignificant.

Seize the opportunity of success to reinforce desirable character traits. Take time to tell your child why you think that success is great. What does it show about the child that can carry over into other areas of life?

You may be able to get extra mileage out of a compliment if you explain how the child's action makes you feel. "Thanks for cleaning your room. It makes me feel good that you are becoming more responsible in taking care of your own things. It makes me feel relieved because it makes less work for me." If your child puts the dirty clothes in the hamper instead of on her floor, you might explain that her new habit makes you happy because it saves you time when you do the laundry.

Wouldn't it be better for your child to understand how his behavior has affected others? He might continue good behavior because he likes being helpful, not just to earn a pat on the head and the assurance that he's "a good boy."

Tell your kids you think they're great just because they're themselves.

Look for those rare, quiet, happy moments when you—inspired by no specific action of your child—can tell him that you love him no matter what, and that you will always love him.

Children with only one parent need to be reassured that you, the remaining parent, will never abandon them (and, when possible, that the absent parent has not abandoned them either).

This reassurance can be effective at the height of success: "Honey, you know how proud I am of you. I want you to know that if you had lost that race, brought home straight *F's*, etc., I'd love you just as much as I do right now. But it sure is great to succeed!"

Reassurance can be effective following failure: "You know I love you no matter what you do. Nothing you could do or say would make me leave you or love you any less." (A child's failures are dealt with in the next chapter.)

Frequently, we assume too much. We think our kids know that we love them, that we won't leave them. But we may be wrong. A little honest conversation and verbalized assurances might relieve some of their fears. Don't be like the guy who declared, "I told that kid I loved him the day he was born. Nothing's changed. If it had, I would have let him know."

Let's make a pact to tell our kids about every greatness we see in them. In a letter to his friend, Philemon, Paul wrote: "I pray that you may be active in sharing your faith, so that you will have a full understanding of every good thing we have in Christ" (Philemon 6).

Help your child discover *every good thing* in him.

Things to Think About/Discuss

1. List your child's areas of greatness. Include skills, gifts, desirable traits, etc.

2. Give three reasonable expectations you have for each of your children. Now give three expectations which might be unreasonable. How does your child react to these expectations?

3. On a scale from 1 to 10, how well do you think you know your child? Why? If possible, ask your child, "On a scale from 1 to 10, how well do you think I know you?"

4. Select five items from question 1, five areas of greatness in your child, and convey your approval to your child today.

5. Make a conscious attempt to "catch your child being good" today. Record your observations.

9

KIDS AREN'T PERFECT

An ugly baby is a very nasty object,
and the prettiest is frightful when undressed.
Queen Victoria

Learning to dislike children at an early age
saves a lot of expense and aggravation later in life.
Robert Byrne

ADMIT IT. THERE ARE THINGS about your kids that are not so great. In fact, don't tell anybody, but there may be times when you don't even like your kids very much. Sure, you love them, but why can't they act like humans at the dinner table? You would never exchange your child for your neighbor's kid, but wouldn't it be nice if *yours* sat still through an entire church service?

When I was still in high school, I spent my summers as a lifeguard and swimming teacher. As it turned out, it was a good thing I held both positions. The first time I undertook the beginners' swimming class, fifty kids showed up. I divided the class, assigned my helpers, and carried out my own duties as instructor and encourager. I tried to get to each child during the first teaching hour to tell him what a fine job he was doing.

"My goodness, you're turning into a real swimmer!" I'd say to a little guy who had worked up enough courage to put his face in the water.

"Look at you! You're swimming!" I'd tell a little girl who dared to take her feet off the bottom of the pool and splash around in two feet of water. I offered great encouragement to all the children.

That afternoon when the pool opened to the public, I was on duty at the deep end. I had to fish out nine little children, all members of my beginners' swim class, to save them from drowning. Convinced that they were already great swimmers, they had confidently jumped off the diving board into the nine-foot deep end only to discover that their teacher had lied to them: they could not swim.

Neglecting to admit failure and weaknesses can be dangerous. If we build false confidences in our children, they may eventually become frustrated and resentful. They may learn to deny anything unpleasant or hard to handle.

Overprotecting our children sets them up for a clash with reality when they leave home and the protective environment. We unintentionally leave them a legacy of lies, or an unhealthy mental filter that carefully deflects all blame from themselves and places it on others. If we cover up their mistakes, we rob them of opportunities to learn by trial and error.

What do we parents do with the "not greats" in our children's lives? I suggest my four-stage plan: 1) prepare for the "not great," 2) face the "not great," 3) accept the "not great," and 4) use the "not great."

Prepare for the Not Great

What you do and say in the positive and neutral zones of childrearing may be your best defense for the negative zones. If you have been fair and generous in praising your child, you will have a better chance of being heard when problems come.

When a child does something that's not great, he needs to know two things: 1. the act was not great, but 2. *he* is still great. We have to be able to separate the child from the things the child does, the doer from the deed.

If you have effectively praised the right stuff in the right way, your child knows you think of him as more than the sum of his acts. You have made it clear that you love him unconditionally, not just because he brought home a good report card. It should logically follow that you still love him now, even though he's brought home a bad report card.

Prepare your child for honesty by being honest yourself. Don't be afraid to admit your own mistakes and faults. Your child will observe how you handle your own "not greats." If you get down on yourself every time you make a mistake, your daughter may have reason to believe you will feel the same toward her when she makes a mistake. If she has never heard about your mistakes and insecurities, if you have never been honest with her about your struggles, she may feel as if she is the only one messing up in an otherwise perfect family.

Recognize that the price of forgiveness has been pre-paid. I think the most powerful tool in building a solid relationship with a child is *pre-paid forgiveness.*

Realize the basis of your own forgiveness. God has forgiven you because he has paid the price for forgiveness with the death of his son Jesus. That high payment is the reason you're forgiven. And you can't earn that forgiveness.

Our children need to know that we love them and forgive them—in advance—for anything "not great" they could ever do. Their acceptance and forgiveness do *not* rest on their performance. When children mess up, they can't be made to fear that they could lose our love. They shouldn't feel they have to earn their way back into our love.

Children should understand that they will receive punishment, consequences, for breaking the rules. But our love and forgiveness should not be affected by anything the children do. It's as if we signed a pre-paid agreement when our children were born into our families. And pre-paid forgiveness is part of the parental package.

Face the Not Great

Denying a problem does not make it go away. John said, "If we claim to be without sin, we deceive ourselves and the truth is not in us" (1 John 1:8).

Andrew had a reading problem. His teacher talked with Andrew's mother about the problem, but Mom disagreed. Her son was a bright boy. If he wasn't doing well in reading, then the teacher must not be doing a good job. "They don't know what they're talking about," she told her son.

Months went by. Andrew never said anything about reading class to his mother. She assumed the teacher had come around and paid more attention to her son. But at the last conference of the year, the teacher told Andrew's mother she would recommend that Andrew repeat first grade. He simply was not ready for second grade.

Laura knew her daughter's teacher had it in for Melissa. There was always some problem, and all because that teacher would not take the time to understand Melissa. Laura suspected that the teacher was jealous of her daughter; all the kids idolized Melissa. In every argument, Laura took her daughter's side. The teacher must be crazy. Melissa would never do the things that teacher said she did. Two years later, Melissa was suspended from classes for destruction of school property.

We are not doing our kids a favor when we refuse to see weaknesses and faults in them. We need to support our kids and believe in them, but not with a blind, ignorant faith. The eyes of love are not blind or myopic, just understanding. We'll never be understanding parents if we refuse to face the *not greats*.

"If we confess our sins, he is faithful and just and will forgive us our sins and purify us from all unrighteousness" (1 John 1:9). We can't confess sins if we refuse to *see* sins.

Accept the Not Great

If you can't accept your child's weaknesses, he will have trouble accepting himself. To demand "great" constantly is to say that "not great" is never permissible. No one can be great in everything he does, unless he is a coward and never ventures into the unknown.

Our children need the freedom to fail. They need to know that *failing* doesn't make them *failures*.

Your children need the freedom to talk to you about their whole world. Do you listen to your daughter talk about friends you don't like? Do you listen to your son as he tells you what a great time he had at his dad's? Is your daughter free to talk about her dates? If you are quick to judge and slow to forgive your child's friends and father, can your child expect you to act any differently with him if he tells you about his mistakes?

Do you force your children (whether consciously or unconsciously) to operate on a "payback" basis? Or are you accepting them unconditionally? Do you hear yourself saying, "How could he do this, after all I've done for him?" If so, that's love on a pay-me-back, conditional system.

When you forgive your daughter for an offense, does she say, "You won't be sorry for this. I'm going to make it up to you"? Does your son feel as if he needs to pay you back in order to earn your love?

You may need to do some serious talking with your children to reestablish a free enterprise system of unconditional love and acceptance. God accepts us because of what Christ did, not because of anything we do. And we need to apply the same standard with our children.

Paul was able to say that he was content with his weaknesses. He knew his thorn in the flesh and could accept it with humility and grace. We need that same attitude about the weaknesses of our children.

Use the Not Greats

Some of my closest times with God have come when I felt I had failed him and myself. It's at those times I'm most tender, more ready to receive his love and instruction. The hard times for our children can provide some of the best opportunities to draw closer to them and to affirm our love. *Use* those times.

Times of failure can also be used to point our children in the direction of success. We might be able to sit down with our children and discuss ways to improve, or prevent a recurrence of the problem. The desire to change and improve is usually at its greatest when the taste of "not great" is fresh.

Accept your kids—their greats and their not-so-greats. Those children are gifts from the Lord.

Things to Think About/Discuss

1. In what ways is your child like you? Unlike you? How do you handle those differences?

2. If you could change one thing about your child, what would it be? Is that change possible? If so, what have you done to bring about that change? How has your child reacted? Prayerfully reevaluate your perception of this dilemma. Do you need to change your approach?

3. List ten positive things you have not given your child credit for. Be on the lookout during the next week for times you can compliment your child and give him credit.

4. How do you react when you make a mistake or fail? How does your child react to his own failures and mistakes? What can you do to promote the freedom to fail in your house?

5. What does it mean to have unconditional love for your children? How can you demonstrate that love?

10

ARE WE HAVING FUN YET?

It is not how much we have,
but how much we enjoy,
that makes happiness.
Charles Spurgeon

My mother had a great deal of trouble with me,
but I think she enjoyed it.
Mark Twain

THE CHRISTMAS AFTER MY divorce, my daughters and I had some tough days. It seemed wrong to decorate the tree by ourselves.

Jenny grew sadder as Christmas approached. The only spark of joy I detected in her came when we saw a commercial on TV for a Pony Nursery for her toy ponies. I would have done anything to make my daughter happy. I scraped my pennies together and bought the present.

Christmas morning when Jenny opened her Pony Nursery, she said, "Thank you," but still seemed depressed.

I was disappointed and angry. "What's it going to take to make you happy, Jenny?" I asked in frustration.

Poor Jenny was as frustrated as I was. "I don't know, Mommy," she cried, "but this isn't it."

What's your favorite emotion? Joy? Happiness? Now, is that favorite emotion the most common in your home? God appointed children to be blessings, bearers of happiness. But we can bury ourselves in our duties so deeply, trying to be both father and mother to our children, that we don't find time to enjoy our kids.

I seem to go through intense states of life when I forget how to have fun. One afternoon in the park, Jenny's grandpa sat on the bench while Jenny and Katy played wildly with any kid who entered the grounds. Jenny suddenly became serious. With a deliberate pace, she walked over to where her grandpa was sitting. "Papa," she said slowly, "Don't you wish merry-go-rounds were still fun for you?"

Merry-go-rounds may never thrill you again, but make an effort to find something you can get excited about with your kids.

Some of us have lost the person with whom we thought we'd live happily ever after. A lot of joy exited with those dreams. But we still have the joy of our children. "Call not that man wretched, who, whatever ills he suffers, has a child to love" (Robert Southey, English poet laureate, 1774-1843).

Killjoys

If children are blessings, why do I feel like crying? Beware of the killjoys. They sit on your shoulder and steal the joy you naturally should have in your children. You can recognize these joy thieves by the sounds they make: *Phooey!; Hmmpff!; Groan-n-n; Grrr!; Sigh; Grunt; Whine.*

Phooey!

By the end of her first week of school in a new kindergarten, Jenny had made many new friends. On Friday, when she came running into the house all excited, I couldn't wait to hear the latest school news.

"Mommy! Mommy! You'll never guess what! Guess what!"

"I don't know, Jenny. I give up. What is it?"

"Alison Sawyer knows how to tie her own shoelaces!"

Phooey! thought I, *and you don't.*

Jenny was thrilled over Alison's accomplishment. She was able to share in that joy. I killed my joy with mental comparisons. *Alison can tie her shoes, but my daughter can't. What's the matter with Jenny? And what's the matter with me? Why is my child the only kid in kindergarten who can't tie her shoelaces?*

I believe joy is the purest, most sincere emotion—joy, that is, for someone else's good fortune. Can you be happy for the kid who gets first place, when your son gets second or fourth?

It is hard for me to see two-parent families enjoying themselves at church or at the park. I don't enjoy other people's anniversary celebrations. But each time I resent their shared joy, or covet it, I am killing my own joy.

Jesus told a parable about laborers in a vineyard. One group of workers had been hired first thing in the morning and had worked all day for a good wage. A second group of workers were hired in the mid-day; and a final group of laborers signed on late in the day.

At the end of the day, all the workers were paid the same wage. Those laborers who had been hired first thing and had worked longest resented the good fortune of the workers hired last. "Why should they get paid the same wage we get, when we had to work all day?" asked the disgruntled laborers.

When the laborers who felt slighted confronted the owner of the vineyard, he had this to say: "Don't I have the right to do what I want with my own money? Or are you envious because I am generous?" (Matthew 20:15).

Are you envious? When you see the success or the lucky breaks of others, does your heart say, "Yippee!" or "Phooey!"? Are you constantly saying, or thinking, "It's not fair! Why does everything good happen to *them*?" Jealousy breeds dissatisfaction and resentment and robs us of joy.

Prescription for the phooey's

We need to change the way we look at gifts. We don't deserve gifts. Neither do other people. Gifts are demonstrations of God's goodness, not our own worthiness.

If you see your ex-spouse living the life you've always dreamed of, even though he or she deserted you and the kids, fight the urge to compare your worth with his net worth. Your ex-partner may have more money, but that has nothing to do with you. All money and gifts are God's to do with as he wishes. We'll probably never understand the why's, but they have nothing to do with personal worth.

Next, focus on the gifts you have, not on the ones you don't have. The laborers in the parable could have chosen to be joyful over the blessings of a good job and fair pay. But they killed their joy by making comparisons. Count your own blessings, and let that consume your time.

The best gifts can't always be seen at first glance. Christmas Eve, Jenny and I sprawled on the floor in front of the Christmas tree to do our last-minute Christmas wrapping.

"Mom," Jenny asked, "Does God have hands and fingers?"

Invoking the art of answering a question with a question (as we parents quickly learn to do when we're out of answers), I responded, "Why do you ask, honey?"

"Because," she explained simply, "I want to give God a Christmas present, but I don't know if he can unwrap it."

We spent the next thirty minutes thinking up presents that didn't need to be unwrapped. They'd be the best gifts, the kind that would reach heaven and wouldn't wear out: kindness, happiness, love, compassion, thoughtfulness.

Those gifts work both ways. Look for all the invisible gifts God has sent your way. Say "Hooray!" to those.

Hmmpff!

Long-term anger or grudges can kill multitudes of joy. The most likely object of your grudge, if you are divorced, is your ex-spouse. But most of us have an array of likely candidates to receive our "hmmpff's."

"The good time my children had at their father's house ends when they cross my threshold," admitted one woman who had been divorced for seven years. "Even if I don't say a word, they know what I'm thinking: *If that man has enough money to take them to a hotel for a week, why do I get such token child support? No wonder his new wife can give them so much attention; she doesn't have to raise kids by herself. Besides, she has more energy since she's ten years younger than I am!*"

"I've been divorced for four years," one mother told me. "Still, every time the kids get sick, or the car breaks down, and I can't pay the bills, I feel like killing that man (her former husband)."

We don't have to go outside our own households to find grudges. "My daughter lied to me once," said a divorced father. "She told me she was delayed at school, when really she had gone off with a friend. She told me the truth later, and she was grounded. But now every time she tells me she is delayed at school, I can't help thinking she's lying again."

"My son was four years old when my wife and I were divorced," complained a discouraged dad. "I have done my best to show him my love. I take him with me as often as our legal visitation allows. We have a good time together, but he still holds the divorce against me. He believes it was all my fault. That is always between us."

Grudges kill joy. Like holding fire in your hand, holding grudges in your heart can burn and consume you.

Prescription for the hmmpff's

Operating under the pre-paid forgiveness principle will help hold down your grudges against your children. If you have committed yourself to forgiving them in advance, it should be easier for you to gain perspective on their actions after-the-fact.

It may be too late to pre-pay forgiveness of your ex-spouse. I admit I still struggle to eradicate bad feelings and grudges. I seem to do better when I focus on what counts—my children, my walk with God—rather than on having a great car or spending money.

Grudges are unproductive; they rarely bother the object of the grudge.

Groan-n-n

Groan is the sound that comes from the single parent as he or she races numbly around the house at 6 A.M., carefully selecting Megan's school clothes, checking to make sure Peter did his homework, trying to give the baby a talking lesson, and hurriedly setting out breakfast.

You may hear this sound again as the single parent brushes through the office building, straightening that three-piece suit, clutching a briefcase, and mentally going over the day's schedule.

Single parents are prime candidates for parental burnout. In the advanced stages of burnout, numbness increases, accomplishments lose their meaning, and relaxing becomes impossible. The only thing the poor single parent has energy left to do is *groan.*

Remedy for the groans

Stop trying to be Superparent. Parents who are highly motivated or idealistic are more likely to put excessive pressure on themselves and their children. You may need to take every thought captive to Christ and check out your values and goals with him. Be open to adjusting your expectations and demands.

Next, live in the present tense. We have to plan for the future. And at times, hope for the future may be the only light we can see from our place in the tunnel. But don't kill the joy of the present by maintaining a constant state of preparation for the future. Enjoy your kids *now.* "Children have neither past nor future; they enjoy the present, which very few of us do" (La Bruyere, *Les Caracteres*).

Tyrone Edwards, a late nineteenth-century American theologian, great-grandson of Jonathan Edwards, wrote:

> Happiness is like manna; it is to be gathered in grains, and enjoyed every day. It will not keep; it cannot be accumulated; nor have we got to go out of ourselves or into remote places to gather it, since it has rained down from Heaven, at our very doors.

Grrrrrrrrr!

No parent likes to admit it, but our own children can rob us of joy when they act like little monsters. If we let our kids get away with murder, is it any wonder they're killing us? As one friend put it,

"Never raise a hand to your children. It leaves the rest of your body unprotected."

Disciplining our children not only helps them develop into better people, it helps us enjoy them. Take a thoughtful look at the qualities or manners in your child which irritate you or infuriate you most often. Can you work with your child to improve in these areas? What can the two of you do to bring more enjoyment and harmony to your home, and cut down on hostile *Grrrrrr's*?

Sigh

"I never have any fun!" complained one mother of two daughters, one in junior high, one in high school. "The girls and I used to have so much fun together after my divorce. We went to the movies together, or stayed home and played games. Now they have their own friends, and I'm home alone every night."

Many single parents lose their married friends. Even if they retain the friendships, they may not be able to spend as much time with them as they used to do. Sooner or later, children will form friendships with kids their own ages. The single parent may sometimes feel left out.

Remedy for the sighs

Don't put all your eggs in your child's basket! That basket becomes too heavy for your child to carry, and you'll end up with scrambled eggs on the floor.

If your children are beginning to find joy and fun with kids their own ages, be happy for them. Share in that joy. Don't make them feel guilty for deserting you.

Members of a single-parent family need to be especially careful about becoming too dependent on each other. A son may be burdened by the premature demand that he become the "man of the house." Daughters may be forced into the role of "little mother." But kids need to be kids, and grown-ups need to be grown-ups.

Develop new friendships. Go to a Sunday school class for single adults. Join Parents Without Partners. Meet a grown-up for lunch or a movie.

Don't depend on your children to meet all your friendship needs. Your child's purpose in life should not be to make you happy.

Grunt!

A grunting sound may be detected coming from single parents who appear to be carrying the weight of the world on their shoulders. A close friend of mine noticed that she seemed to undergo a personality change when she entered her house after work each day. At work she was the Funny Lady, ready for a laugh, the life of the office. But when she walked through her own doors, she took off her coat and put on her burdens. One especially burdensome evening, her third-grader surprised her with an innocent question: "Mom, Carolyn's mother said you were really funny at the office. Why don't you ever laugh at home?"

Yokes and jokes

Christ offers a good trade—our yokes for his.

> Come to me, all you who are weary and burdened, and I will give you rest. Take my yoke upon you and learn from me, for I am gentle and humble in heart, and you will find rest for your souls. For my yoke is easy and my burden is light. *Matthew 11:28-30*

Trade yokes. When the early Hebrews crossed a threshold, they made a sign of peace before entering. Imagine yourself making the peaceful exchange of yokes each time you cross your home threshold. Give the weight of your world to Christ.

Try being funny with your kids. My friend said it had never occurred to her to clown around at home like she did at work. It took some practice, but she discovered her children's soft spots for humor. For her youngest child, funny faces did the trick. Her oldest daughter appreciated a good joke. She was almost ready to give up on her middle child when she discovered that laughter begat laughter. If she began to laugh, soon he couldn't help but laugh, too.

If you have a good sense of humor, use it. If you don't, try to develop one. Laughter still makes pretty good medicine.

Whine...

Nothing squelches joy faster than self-pity. I've said it before: Single parents make wonderful martyrs. It comes so naturally with the territory.

On an old TV show called "Queen for a Day," contestants told their sad stories and hardships to the audience. Then audience applause was measured, and the contestant who drew the most applause for her depressing story was awarded a cash prize. I've always believed I could match anyone with my tales of martyrdom.

Heartfelt whines may be heard when the martyr addresses the past, present, or future. Whines over the past sound something like this: "When I was married, I used to go out to a nice restaurant at least once a week. Sometimes I'd even buy a dress that wasn't marked for final clearance."

Present-tense whines go more like this: "I'm almost forty. All I do is work, take care of kids, work, take care of kids, work, etc. I have $26 to last until payday. The rent is due; my car needs new tires. None of this is fair. I shouldn't have to live like this. And do these kids appreciate all I'm sacrificing for them? Of course not."

Future whines take various forms. "I'll never be happy again. The best is behind me. I have nothing to look forward to, nothing to live for."

Adjust your focus.

Perspective determines how you see. I used to live near a busy intersection. Every time I drove through that intersection, I got mad at pedestrians who paid no attention to traffic signals. Each time I traversed the intersection on foot, I got mad at drivers who raced through the yellow light.

One day Jenny caught on to me. "Mommy, how come every time we drive here, there are crazy walkers, but whenever we walk, there are crazy drivers?" Same circumstances, different perspectives.

When you look over your past, remember the times when good things happened to you. But be happy again about those experiences, instead of letting them give you regrets about your current circumstances. Use those blessings as a healthy reminder that God has always come through for you.

Enjoy the present. You'll never have the gift of that moment again. Each new stage of life, for us and for our children, is an adventure.

We can be hopeful about the future when we focus on Christ. If our hope is in anything else, we probably will be disappointed. But Romans 5:5 promises, "And hope does not disappoint us, because God has poured out his love into our hearts by the Holy Spirit, whom he has given us."

Turn the focus away from yourself. Take the kids to visit a nursing home and "adopt" someone who is lonely. Make it a family project to support a starving child in a third-world country for a small monthly charge. Do *something* unselfish. It cuts down on the whines.

We want our children to be happy. Children usually take their cues from their parents, although sometimes it works the other way around. Four-year-old Jenny came home from preschool in tears one morning.

"Jenny, what's the matter?" I asked.

Jenny tried to stop the sobs. "Christopher says *he* lives in a house, and we only live in a 'partment."

More sobs, and then: "We don't live in a 'partment, do we, Mommy? We live in a home!" Then again, with a big grin, "We live in a home."

Up until that moment, I had basically agreed with Christopher. I wanted a *house*. But as I hugged Jenny, I agreed that I was pretty happy with our *home*.

What is it going to take to make *you* happy?

Things to Think About/Discuss

1. On a scale of 1 to 10 (where 1 = no fun, and 10 = a never-ending party), how much fun would you say you have with your children? Now ask your kids the same question.

2. What habits or rough edges do your children have that make them harder to enjoy? Decide which habits you can help them overcome and which you may need to accept.

3. Think of any outstanding grudges you are holding. How do these grudges affect your joy? What can you do today to get rid of those grudges?

4. What unselfish action can you take to turn your family's focus away from its own problems to help others who are less fortunate? Talk with your children and decide on a family project.

5. List two things you will do this week to have fun with your children. Now think up two things you will do this week to have fun without your children. You'll be surprised how alone-time helps relieve parent-burnout.

PART III

FOR EVERY COMPLEX QUESTION,
THERE IS A SIMPLE ANSWER—
AND IT IS ALWAYS WRONG.

11

TRUTH OR CONSEQUENCES

I believe in telling the truth.
If you tell the truth,
you don't have to remember so much.
Mark Twain

SINGLE-PARENTING IS A COMPLIcated business. When I found myself alone, with custody of my children, I wondered if I could really pull this one off and keep us all alive. Everything was hard. It was hard to find enough work to support my family. It was hard to make so many decisions alone. It was hard to know what to tell my daughters about our new life or about their father.

Easy Answers?

When things are hard, easy answers seem enticing. When a friend urged me to move and start all over in a new city, I was ready to grab on to that advice. But when another friend shared her conviction that change adds to the current distress, she sounded just as convincing.

I agreed with my relatives who said I should stop blaming myself and quit trying to understand where I went wrong. But I also agreed with friends who encouraged me to look inside and deal with what had gone wrong.

I was given a book that made a good case for putting myself first, getting my act together, and taking time for myself. It sounded good—until I read a book from my shelves about the needs of children of divorce. That author made a strong case for the single parent to do whatever it takes to convince children that they are of primary importance to their parents.

As sole parent in the house, I needed to decide on a party line of discipline. Should I buckle down or back off? Advice flowed freely from both camps.

And just how much truth did I owe my children about the divorce? Would the details of the break-up destroy their image of their father? Or would it be worse for them to find out ugly details from someone else later? Everyone had a different opinion on the subject.

In the musical *Fiddler on the Roof*, Tevye, the lovable Papa, usually manages to see both sides of an issue. When two men argue heatedly, Tevye listens to the first man and says, "He is right." Then he listens to the second man and pronounces, "He is also right." When a third peasant tells Tevye, "Friend, these two men cannot both be right," Tevye responds, "You are also right."

As Tevye argues within himself to reconcile his traditions with the changing world, he reasons, "On the one hand..." and, "On the other hand ..." supplying both sides of the argument with convincing rationale.

Much of life comes in two-handed packages: On the one hand, this seems right. On the other hand, that seems right. Jesus said,

"He who is not *with* me is *against* me" (Matthew 12:30, italics mine). But he also said, "Whoever is not *against* us is *for* us" (Mark 9:40, italics mine).

Solomon wrote about a time to tear down and a time to build up, a time to weep and a time to laugh, a time to mourn and a time to dance, a time to throw stones and a time to gather stones, a time to embrace and a time to shun embracing, a time to search and a time to give up as lost, a time to keep and a time to throw away, a time to tear apart and a time to sew together, a time to be silent and a time to speak, a time to love and a time to hate, a time to be silent and a time to speak, a time to love and a time to hate, a time for war and a time for peace. (See Ecclesiastes 3.)

I once knew a family who had a *welcome* mat which read, "Beware of Dogs." Talk about contradictions!

Life doesn't come in neat parcels with easy-to-follow directions. Part Three is dedicated to those complexities inherent in single-parenthood. Each of the next four chapters examines a major problem or decision we have to make. We'll give both sides of the question a fair look and try to set some guidelines to help you make your own decisions, using the available advice. "For lack of guidance a nation falls, but many advisers make victory sure" (Proverbs 11:14).

What Should I Say?

Mother and Father have decided to divorce. What should they tell the children? A single mother who has never married is asked by her son to tell him about his father. How does she answer? A widow who has kept several secrets from her daughter is afraid the truth about her father's suicide will come out. What *do* we tell our children about their other parent or about ourselves?

Details

On the one hand, we need to tell it like it is. We owe our kids the truth. They need to hear the truth and nothing but the truth from us—before they hear it from someone else. One article advised:

> Children are literal...They have trouble with euphemisms, and may misunderstand. For example, when you say, "I have bad news, darling, we lost Grandpa," they might turn right around and say: "Well, let's go look for him." So, give them all the details. (Michael O'Malley, *The Single Parent*, March/April 1987)

On the other hand, a different article in the same magazine, "Spell It Out for Your Children," offered this advice: "Don't overload your children with too much information too quickly" (*The Single Parent*, March/April 1987).

And in the same issue of *The Single Parent*: "Be general when telling the children what's happening. They don't understand adult terms like 'separation' and 'spite.' Just say you will always love them and be there for them."

What We Both Want?

On the one hand, we need to help our children face and accept their new circumstances realistically. It won't help them if we lie and tell them that divorce will be the best for everybody when actually we don't feel it's best for them to live without a father. It isn't honest to convince children that the father they've never seen really does love them.

In his book *How to Single Parent*, Dr. Fitzhugh Dodson writes:

> I'd like to elaborate now on what I said earlier about telling the children the truth. It's natural in some situations for the initiator of the divorce to want to withhold his or her identity from the children. He's afraid if the children know who wanted the divorce he will immediately be cast into the role of Bad Guy. So he tries to give the children the impression that both parents mutually wanted to separate. But that won't wash. The children will very quickly figure out who wanted the divorce and who didn't. So it's much better to tell them the truth, even if he goes through a temporary period of being labeled Mr. Bad Guy (or Mrs. Bad Guy). Only the truth will guarantee the credibility of the parents.

On the other hand, children need to maintain love and respect for both parents. The custodial single parent should do all he or she can to promote a positive image of the absent parent. Children feel deeply that they are a part of both of their parents. If they lose respect for one of their parents, they may suffer from low self-esteem for years, if not for life.

"I operate on a *need-to-know* basis with my kids," wrote one single dad. "Why should I tell them ugly details about their mother's affairs when they don't need to know?"

A young mother who had never been married stated: "I've told my daughter that her father *does* love her, even though I am sure he does not. How could a six-year-old girl possibly stand to hear that her own father doesn't love her? It's easier for my daughter to believe that her father loves her but has other problems."

"I have been divorced for fifteen years," wrote one mother. "I have never told my children the horrible things their father did to me. I'm sure it's the right decision."

These parents try to tell the truth selectively.

How Do You Feel?

On the one hand, you need to be honest about your feelings and emotions when you talk with your children. If your children can see you grieve, they may feel freer to show you their grief.

If you put up a brave front, a stiff upper lip, you present a model of dishonesty for your children to follow. They may try to be "brave little soldiers," keeping their anger and pain inside, and thus prolonging the grieving process.

Let the kids see you as you are, so that you can see them as they are. "The child's grief throbs against its little heart as heavily as the man's sorrow" (E.H. Chapin, 1814-80, American clergyman).

On the other hand, children are not adults. They *do* need our protection. We have a responsibility to help make their adjustment as smooth as possible.

The following quotes from Marie Winn's book, *Children Without Childhood,* illuminate a changing relationship between adults and children:

> Something has happened to blur the formerly distinct boundaries between childhood and adulthood, to weaken the protective membrane that once served to shelter children from precocious experience and sorrowful knowledge of the adult world. All over the country newly single mothers are sitting down with their children and making what has come to be known as *The Speech*: "Look, things are going to have to be different. We're all in this together, and we're going to have to be partners."

> ...as today's children impress adults with their sophisticated ways, adults begin to change their ideas about children and their needs; that is they form new conceptions of childhood. Why, these tough little customers don't require protection and careful

> nurture! No longer need adults withhold information about the harsh realities of life from children. No longer need they hide the truth from children. No longer need they hide the truth about their own weaknesses. Rather, they begin to feel it is their duty to prepare children for the experiences of modern life. However, as adults act less protectively...and as they expose children to the formerly secret underside of their lives ... those former innocents grow tougher, perforce, less playful and trusting, more skeptical—in short, more like adults (pp. 4,6-7).

Answering the Why's

One fourteen-year-old boy was called into the counselor's office for disruptive classroom behavior. During his talk with the counselor, he said this: "I know I caused my parents' divorce. They're good people, and they've never given me any other reason why they got a divorce. So I know it was my fault." That boy was only eighteen months old when his parents divorced.

What about telling a child of divorce why his parents are divorcing? Is the cause something a child *needs* to know? On the one hand, a child whose home is being broken apart deserves an explanation.

But some parents evade talking to their kids about the causes of their divorce because they believe the children have no idea about any of the unpleasant truths. However, children are frequently smarter than we imagine. Ogden Nash wrote the following in a poem entitled, "What Makes the Sky Blue?":

> Oh what a tangled web do parents weave
> When they think that their children are naive.

On the other hand, divorce is between adults. Therefore, many feel that the contention and disputes should be restricted to the parents. Children may not be emotionally and mentally mature enough to understand the causes of their parents' divorce.

Maybe the parents themselves barely understand the causes. Dodson, in *How to Single Parent*, says:

> As to what causes divorce, I think it is fruitless to speculate... What I am saying is that there are so many permutations and combinations of personality factors which lead to a breakup that it is futile to try to figure out what "caused" a divorce (p. 15).

When I first had to tell Jenny and Katy that their father would no longer be living with us, I searched Scripture and weighed both sides. I discovered Proverbs 14:8: "The folly of fools is deception." But I also realized that even truth can be destructive and must be handled with care and reserve. "Set a guard over my mouth, O LORD; keep watch over the door of my lips" (Psalm 141:3). I felt that Katy and Jenny needed to know the basic why's so they would understand that Daddy was leaving and wouldn't be back. But I spared them all the "dirty details" that I felt would be damaging to them personally and to their view of their father now and in the future.

Which Way to Turn?

We want our children to trust us, to feel secure and loved. A good case can be made for telling your child the whole truth; a good case can also be made for withholding truth from your child.

Unfortunately, this isn't the place where I hand you a neat solution, complete with all the right answers you'll ever need. I wish I could. Life would be easier if we were handed more answers. But I think God is interested in the process of our decision-making, our moment-by-moment reliance on him to show us which way to go, to convict us when we've made the wrong move. God has given us his Spirit, the Spirit of Truth, unknown by the world. Ultimately, you will have to decide what to tell your children. Be sensitive to their reactions and to God's conviction.

Make a list of *truths* about your present singleness: your divorce, your relationship with your spouse before he/she died, your decision not to marry. Include truths about the absent parent and about yourself. Which of these have you communicated to your children? Which are still secrets?

Now, consider whether your truths fit into any of the categories of truth that follow. This exercise may help you decide what you need to tell your children.

Anticipated truth

Anticipate your child's needs, and make sure you give him enough information to quell his worst fears. The two biggest fears for most children of divorce are: 1. What will become of me when Mom and Dad split up? and 2. Am I somehow to blame for the breakup?

Fears of children who have lost a parent through death are similar: 1. Will I lose my remaining parent? and 2. Was it my fault? Those two questions, even if not expressed verbally, need truthful answers.

Jenny was barely four years old when her father and I separated. I had read how children blame themselves in a divorce, but I didn't believe it applied in my case. Jenny had given me no reason to believe she was blaming herself.

Then in the middle of the night, about six months after the separation, Jenny climbed into bed with me and poked me awake.

"Mommy," she whispered, "I figured out why Daddy left us. He likes boys better than girls." Jenny knew that her father was seeing a woman who had little boys. I knew she needed to know more of the truth.

So tell your children enough of the truth to keep them from concluding it's all their fault.

A mother may find it hard to talk with her children about their father, especially if she feels he has deserted the family. Still, children need to know enough about their dad to keep them from worrying about him. It's usually best if children can see where their father now lives. Don't assume they know the obvious; young children can believe that their father has disappeared. Or they might worry that he is walking around aimlessly with no home.

Katy was one year old when her father left us. The only times she saw her dad during the next two years were when he traveled by train to spend a couple of days with the girls in a motel. It took nearly two years to convince Katy that her father did not inhabit every train we saw.

Ongoing truth

I used to think "telling the children about the divorce" referred to the "big talk," the time when the parent(s) sit down with their children to inform them about the pending divorce. But *telling* can't be done in one sitting. Don't expect that you're done when you've given out your information.

Your children will have more unanswered questions as they work through the shock phase of grief. Be available for them. They may ask the same questions over and over, trying to understand. They may develop new questions as they grow older. Hopefully, you will see things more clearly with time and can make matters clearer to them.

Balanced truth

One help you can provide for your children is to give them a perspective on their circumstances. Children haven't lived long enough to have developed a feel for the past or the future. Without giving them false hopes, describe your goals and plans for the future. Help them put the past in perspective. You *did* have good times as a two-parent family, but you also had hard times.

Play fair. Strive for a balance in your truth. If you tell your son about your ex-spouse's affair, don't forget to tell him about your own failures in your marriage. A good test is to ask yourself, "Could I tell this truth to my child if his other parent were in the room with us?" Be careful with the truth. Matthew 12:36 says, "Men will have to give account on the day of judgment for every careless word they have spoken."

Bearable truth

Once Jesus said to his disciples, "I have many more things to say to you, but you cannot bear them now" (John 13:12). You need to know your child in order to discern how much truth is bearable. Don't forget, truth is ongoing. It is possible to deliver it in different portions, and at varying speeds, depending on the child's readiness to receive the truth. She may want to know more at sixteen than she did when she was only eight.

God is truth. Since we're dealing in his territory, with his children, we need to keep in close communion with him.

Things to Think About/Discuss

1. List three truths about your singleness, three truths about yourself, and three truths about the other parent. Circle the truths you have *not* discussed with your children. Consider each circled truth separately. Do you feel you need to talk to your children about any of these issues? If so, when and how do you plan to do it?

2. Have you said anything to your children about your life with their other parent that you wish you had not discussed? Is there anything you can do to lessen the damage?

3. Predict what you think your child will answer when you ask him, "What caused my divorce?" (If you are widowed, perhaps you could ask your child what he understands about his parent's death. If you've never married, you might ask your child to tell you why she thinks you remained unmarried.) Next go and ask the kids. How accurate were your predictions? Any surprises?

4. Do you feel children at times need to be protected from the truth? If so, when—and how?

12

ME FIRST OR LAST?

AS A SINGLE PARENT, ONE OF THE tough decisions you have to make is whether to put yourself first or last on your priority list. You're not sure exactly where you should fit—or where you want to fit. Let's find out. Score yourself on the following quiz:

0	1	2	3	4
Never	Seldom	Sometimes	Often	Always

___ 1. I leave my kids with a sitter (or relative) so I can have some fun on my own.

___ 2. My needs are more important than my children's needs.

___ 3. If I want to date someone my children don't like, I go ahead and date him/her.

___ 4. My children understand when I want privacy or time alone.

___ 5. My kids are happy for me when I go somewhere fun without them.

___ 6. I have newer and nicer clothes than my children do.
___ 7. I am involved in more activities than my kids are.
___ 8. If I get a vacation, we will go where *I* want to go.
___ 9. If my children and I watch TV, we watch what I want to see.
___ 10. My kids pitch in and do their share of work at home.

There are forty points possible. If you've scored 25-40 on this unscientific quiz, you may tend to put yourself first. If you scored 0-15, your kids may be coming in first. And if you've scored 16-24, you must be a Superparent—you've got a great balance in priorities.

Priorities

What should be the priorities of a single-parent family? At a gathering of single parents, this question usually stirs some heated discussion. Here's what two single moms had to say:

> *I put my kids first, at least ahead of me: God, my kids, myself and others.*
>
> Sure, that sounds great and noble, but it doesn't work. If I'm not together, how can I help my children? God, myself, and then my children—those are my priorities.
>
> *The Bible tells us, "Do nothing out of selfish ambition or vain conceit, but in humility consider others better than yourselves" (Philippians 2:3).*
>
> But Jesus also said, "Love your neighbor as yourself." Now, how can I love my neighbor or my children unless I love myself first?

And the apostle Paul told us that with other people, including our children, we should "honor one another above yourselves" (Romans 12:10). That's what I'm doing—giving preference to my kids.

Paul also wrote that each of us is a temple of the living God. I have a responsibility to care for my temple. If I don't put myself first, my kids will trod all over this temple!

All I know is that children of divorce (or children lacking a parent for whatever reason) suffer terribly. My kids need all the love and time I can give them at this crucial time. They have never needed me more. I have less time than I used to have, and I'm all my kids have now. So I have to give them what little free time I do get.

Children with only one parent need that parent to be healthy and strong. I won't be healthy if I give my kids all my free time. I need a life of my own.

Okay, let's consider the effect of priorities on our kids. Mine have just been deserted, rejected by their father. They need to feel they're important to me, that I want to be with them. And they understand my actions better than my words. I can say, "I love you and you mean the world to me," but if I leave them every chance I get, they'll feel rejected by me, too. Isn't it enough that they have to be in daycare and with sitters now that I've gone back to work full-time? Do I have to leave them with a sitter on the weekend, too?

Okay, but what about the effect of priorities on my children? If I make my kids the center of my world, is that really best for them? I don't want them growing up believing other people's

> lives revolve around them. I don't want them to follow in my self-appointed martyr steps and learn to sacrifice themselves and their personal happiness.

Are you confused yet? Let's check out what the experts say about home priorities.

Me First

In *Coping with Being Single Again*, J. Clark Henley writes:

> Avoid a completely child-oriented home. As a single parent, you may tend to be overprotective or overpermissive and allow your home to become completely child-oriented. To do so is unfair and unhealthy for all involved (p. 89).

Another author made this point against putting children ahead of self: You're not helping your child when you make him the center of life any more than two parents help a child when they put him ahead of their marriage relationship. Two parents must consider their relationship as top priority. A single parent must consider her relationship with herself as her top priority. Ultimately, that's the best thing she can do for her child.

As parents, and especially as single parents, we must learn to emphasize "quality" attention over "quantity" attention. Instead of pressuring ourselves to spend two solid hours with each child each weeknight (and then trying to get the wash, dishes, and lawn cleaned up during the *same* two hours!), try spending a half hour of concentrated time. Attend only *to* that child. Read a book together, or talk about his day. A few hours spent each week with a healthy, happy, whole parent are worth more than many hours spent with a worn and frazzled parent.

Dr. Fitzhugh Dodson writes, "As a single parent your first priority is yourself. You must learn to rid yourself of guilt and become 'creatively selfish.' "

Sacrificial mothers sometimes struggle with the martyr attitude. An article in a 1985 issue of *Single Parent Magazine* argued that sacrificial mothers build guilt into their children. Spoken or unspoken, the message is clear: *Nobody around here appreciates me. After all I've done for you, the least you could do is...*

I think every single parent has felt that way some time in his or her parenting experience. The need for "me" time is very important, especially in sorting out issues about personal self-worth and esteem after the divorce.

Me Last

On the other hand, much can be said about putting yourself last. Most children in divorced families struggle with big questions about themselves and their families. They wonder why their family has to be different from their best friends'. Why can't Mom and Dad get along? Secretly, many children hope Mom and Dad will get back together. Other children feel guilty because they are glad the shouting and fighting have stopped.

Children may feel lost (and unloved by the departing parent). They need a truckload of love, patience, and understanding. Parents with open eyes and hearts can really help them adjust.

In *Finding Your Place After Divorce*, Carole Sanderson Streeter argues for children first:

> Any good mother often puts the needs of her children ahead of her own. As an adult, you can delay gratification of your own needs. Children don't have much capacity for this... They need attention now to their emotional needs.

> For you as a divorced mother, home is the primary place where you will sacrifice for others. Sacrifice is an old-fashioned word that has gone out of style, even in Christian circles... Sacrifice has never been popular. It is not easy to put aside your own preferences and needs and give to other people. And yet that is what all Christians are called to do.
>
> Some people think it is unhealthy for a single parent to sacrifice her needs in favor of the child.... The tone of the world today is that gratification should not be delayed, that an adult needs satisfaction now. That the adult is more important than the child... (p. 73).

Our world is very "me" centered. You can realize this by watching TV advertisements for just one moment: If I use that cologne, I'll have the best-looking date; that toothpaste will give me a sexy smile, etc. Very rarely do the commercials say, "Stay home tonight. Your child needs you." Or, "Have you hugged your child today?"

In this person-eat-person world, it's easy to climb the rungs of the personal success ladder (whether success means clothes, contacts, or power), not realizing you are stepping on your child's fingers along the way. William Thompson honestly identifies his own struggle in this area: "I am becoming much too self-centered. I worry about myself all the time."

The Precarious Balance

I suppose all of life is a struggle for balance, but I think we single parents face the most difficult balancing act of all. Children, career, friends, romance (or lack thereof), finances, home, etc. are hard enough for two parents to balance. Take away half the work force, and you're left balancing in a dangerous position. Then, just when you think you've regained your balance, someone throws you another ball to juggle. So don't be too hard on yourself if you find yourself toppling off-balance.

I think we can agree that we want to put God first and the family second. But those priorities demand hard choices. I need to put God first. But do I attend a church I like, even though the kids prefer one I don't like? Do I take a daily half hour of personal worship time when the laundry's piled up and we need groceries and the girls want me to play Barbies with them?

Priorities have to be temporarily rearranged at times. If one child is sick, you may have to neglect the other children a little. You may have to settle for being a good teacher instead of a great teacher, or an average student instead of an impressive one, because you don't have time to prepare thoroughly. If there is a short-term project that requires excellence from you, you may need to take some of the kids' time and pour it into that project. That doesn't mean you've changed your priorities. You've just temporarily rearranged them. And that's between you and God.

We single parents run a high risk of making our families self-centered. With so many pressures in a single-parent home, we may not have time to think about the needs of those outside the home. Yet looking to the needs of others usually helps us put our own needs in perspective. Try taking the kids with you to visit the elderly in a nursing home. Ask a local hospital or orphanage or nursing home if you can bring cookies in and put on a little Christmas or Easter program. Commit yourself to visit the people there regularly.

Be sensitive to indications that you've crossed the balance line of priorities. When I see myself hovering over my children and trying to control every move they make, I just think about the lesson my daughter Katy has taught me through her stormy relationship with our Allyson J. Cat.

Katy has given new meaning to the phrase "killing with kindness." She loves that mongrel, Allyson J. Cat. In fact, several times she has nearly loved Ali Cat to death. One morning I walked into the living room to find Katy sitting on a pillow and sporting a huge grin. The pillow was on top of Ali Cat. Katy only wanted to hide Ali so she could keep her to herself.

Katy is so devoted to Allyson J. that she squeezes her with love. And for all this love and adoration, what does Katy receive in return? Allyson J. Cat runs away when she sees Katy coming.

We can be like that with our children; we can drive them away with our possessive, destructive love. We can make them our top priority, but smother them with immature love.

On the other hand, I can usually count on my other daughter Jenny to remind me that she comes before my work. Last summer I was scheduled to speak to a large group of aspiring writers in Chicago: "Everything You Need to Know about Nonfiction Books, From Start to Finish." And on my desk lay the only notes I'd prepared for my lectures, two handwritten pages. I *had* to get some work done.

Slowly, silently, a small hand turned the doorknob to my office and pushed open the door. Jenny crossed the forbidden territory to my desk and slid onto my lap.

Frustrated with all I had to do, I blurted out, "How many times have I told you not to interrupt me when I'm working? What do you want?"

Jenny slid off my lap as quietly as she had climbed up. But before leaving, she looked over her shoulder and said, "I didn't want anything. I just wanted to be with you." You can imagine how I felt after that simple, humble, loving statement!

Kids need to be with us. We need to provide the security, the assurance that we think they are very important.

Things to Think About/Discuss

1. Reread the dialogue between single moms. Which mom do you tend to agree with?

2. What do you think of Dr. Dodson's advice to become "creatively selfish"? How does this apply to your children? To you?

3. Name the different "balls" you juggle in your personal balancing act. Underline any items you feel are demanding too much of your resources. What can you do to rearrange the balance?

4. Name three things you have done for people outside your immediate family in the last month. Plan one outing or project you can do with your children to focus on needs outside your family.

5. List five things you can do this week to show your children how important they are to you.

13

BUCKLE DOWN OR BACK OFF?

In this world, there are only two tragedies.
One is not getting what one wants;
and the other is getting it.
Oscar Wilde

DISCIPLINE IS ANOTHER TOPIC single parents are divided over. The following is an example of the differences that have been expressed as I've listened to groups of singles. You may find yourself agreeing with one of them.

Moderator: You have all been single parents for about a year now, and I'd like to ask your advice on discipline in the single-parent family. First, what advice do you have for new single parents? How should they handle their children during those first few critical weeks and months?

Cheryl: My kids had lost their security and a big chunk of their happiness. I did everything I could to help them regain their happiness. We spent more time together, did fun things. As far as discipline goes, I backed off and let them do what they wanted. They didn't need me to make their world tougher—it was tough enough.

Marsha: I disagree with Cheryl. Kids need security when their world falls apart. And discipline brings security. I buckled down, set the rules early, and made them stick. The kids may not always have been happy about our "tight ship," but in the long run, it was what they needed.

Moderator: Well, what about now? Do you still feel you need to hold such tight control, or can you ease off a bit?

Dan: Marsha's right. You have to buckle down. Kids need to learn obedience. If they don't learn it at home, where will they learn it?

Jeff: I don't think so. If you give kids so many rules, and keep checking on them, how will they ever learn independence from you? What will they do when they get out in the world where no one watches over them to make sure they're keeping the rules?

These statements pose big questions for the single parent: What effect will our method of discipline have on our children now *and* later? We want them to be responsible, honest grown-ups. We want them to be close-to-perfect models for the human race—individuals we will be proud of when we are grandparents.

Cheryl uses the measure of time in the future to help her parent in the present:

Cheryl: Jeff's right! I apply the "20-year-rule" with my kids: "Will this matter in twenty years?" If it will, then I take it more seriously. If it won't, then I get a better perspective on the situation.

Marsha: But you have to make each day count. You may never have another opportunity like the one in front of you. Everything *is* serious.

Cheryl: You can't go around believing everything is serious! Your kids have enough pressures without you making home a pressure, too.

Parenting is serious business. There are pressures on both parents and kids to get along. But far too often we make parenting just that—*business*. We buy and sell our children's creativity just to make them "normal" and "acceptable to our way of doing things. When an eight-year-old clowns around, his dad yells at him, "Get serious, Danny! I'm not raising a circus performer! I want you to do something with your life!" So Danny becomes a serious (and dull!) adult in order to meet Dad's requirements. Jeff talks about kids who please parents:

Jeff: Really—otherwise your kids get hyper about pleasing you. They'll do anything so they won't fall out of favor with the one parent they have left. I know a single mom like that. Everybody thinks her daughter is so well-behaved. But that poor kid is too well-behaved. She isn't going to chance losing her mom, too.

Dan: Well, I know too many kids with only one parent who are used to getting their own way. Or they play one parent off the other because both are afraid of disciplining and displeasing the child.

Dan has a valid point, too. All of us have seen a mom struggle with her screaming child in the grocery store. You just know the child is used to having his own way. And that manipulation-punishment cycle is hard to break. It's even harder for single parents, who sometimes hesitate to discipline a child, afraid to alienate all that's left of the "family" or fearing that the child will go live with the other parent.

But the parent is responsible for the child. This raises the moderator's next question:

Moderator: One of you mentioned "responsibility." What is the best way to help children become responsible people?

Jeff: You build responsibility by giving freedoms, letting kids make mistakes. I used to teach at a Christian college. I knew kids who had been great at home—where Mom and Dad made all the rules and made sure the rules were strictly observed. But when those kids hit college and got a few freedoms, they went crazy! They couldn't handle the independence.

Dan: But responsibility doesn't just happen; it's learned. It's our duty to build responsibility in our children through calculated discipline. At first I give my son a chore and make sure he does it. I have to follow through and check up on him. Then by the time it's a habit and he does that chore without my reminding him, it's become a responsibility.

Cheryl: I refuse to be the bad guy all the time. Since my divorce, my children and I have become best friends. We're closer than I ever thought possible.

Marsha: Children don't need another buddy. They need a parent.

Jeff: But a parent who can laugh and have fun with them.

Dan: Yeah—a parent who can be tough, but loving, too.

Moderator: Okay. So what you're saying is this: There are times when we need to buckle down, but there are other times when we should back off. We just have to be sharp enough to figure out which is which.

Parents can realize that there is a time for being serious and a time for laughing. Our lives would be threadbare without both. We need to be both parents and friends, guardians and playmates, to our children.

Discipline

Discipline is one of the hardest assignments for the single parent. Not only does she have less time to spend in parenting, the single parent has lost the system of checks and balances. There's no one around to catch her operating in her blind spots. No one is immediately present to say, "Come on, you're nagging at the boy." Or, "It's not that big a deal. You're not listening to her." No one is there to help enforce the family rules.

The non-custodial parent may have an even tougher time with discipline. He doesn't want to spend his few weekends playing truant officer with his son. Or he may feel the frustration of having only scattered days throughout the year to discipline his teenage daughter as he feels she needs to be disciplined.

Who's on First?

Anything with multiple heads is a monster—including families. Someone in your family has to be the head of the household; and as a single parent, you're it. You don't need to be the dictator, or even a benevolent king. But you do need to keep a healthy balance between authority and love. The "loving authority" environment provides a sense of security for your child.

Many single-parent homes have achieved a spirit of cooperation through shared decision-making, family councils, and divided responsibilities. But the ultimate security rests on the parent functioning as the head of the family. When the parent ceases to fill that role, anything can happen.

"I've lost it," one single mom with three children told me. "My son goes out when he wants to and comes in when he wants to. He doesn't listen to me anymore. It's frightening!"

"My life is a series of responses to the urgent pleas of my daughters," said another mother. " 'Mom, I have to go here.' Or, 'Mom, I need this, and I've got to have it *now*!' " All of us can identify with this harassed mom.

A non-custodial father complained, "I don't know what to do with my five-year-old daughter. I love her, but her mother is ruining her by giving her anything she wants, never saying no to anything. My daughter runs that household—not my ex-wife!"

The first sentence of Dr. Logan Wright's book, *Parent Power: A Guide to Reasonable Childrearing*, says, "The order of the day for any parent who wants to return some semblance of sanity is to get and maintain control." That is what the mother with the screaming toddler needs to do when he strews his Tupperware toys all over the living room floor. She needs to take firm charge of that young life. But not all experts agree with Dr. Wright on the subject of discipline.

Dr. Fitzhugh Dodson writes, "Be as relaxed as you can. Having a minimum of rules for him to rebel against is always good advice for this stage. But it is especially wise when your first (i.e. your child) is going through the stress of divorce" (*How to Single Parent*, p. 98).

So now you're really confused. You've got evidence on both sides for what others think is best. But what's best for *you*? *And* your children?

Motives

Your *method* of discipline is probably not as crucial as the *motive* for your actions. Anatole Broyard shares,

> There was a time when we expected nothing of children but obedience, as opposed to the present, when we expect everything of them but obedience (*Books of the Times*, p. 333).

Let's look at the reasons why we turn to a particular method when faced with a discipline problem. Whether you tend to back off or buckle down, you need to examine your reasons for choosing that method.

Know why you are backing off

How can we know when to loosen the reins and ease up on our children? It may help to run a motive check on yourself. If your motive for lightening discipline is one of the following, it's time for a change.

Pity. Beware of the "poor, poor, pitiable me" rationale at work in your children or in yourself. Do you give in to their demands, spend money on them beyond your means, or give them extra privileges just because you feel sorry for them?

It's natural to feel sorry for your children; they do miss a lot by having only one parent. But you're not helping them if you teach them they can get what they want by making others feel sorry for them. Martyr complexes can follow them all their lives.

Popularity. If you hear that inner voice whisper, "I'd better let him have his way or he won't like me very much," don't listen to it. If you think, "I know their father lets them do this, and I don't want them to like him more than they like me," think again. Popularity isn't worth spoiling your children. God never promised parents popularity.

Pooped. I'm afraid some of us are just too tired to follow through on our principles. If you recognize this pattern of giving in because you're too pooped to argue, something needs to change. Decide what you can handle in advance, *before* you're worn out.

Know why you are buckling down

When is it a mistake to buckle down? If your tight discipline is motivated by one of the following, it's time to reevaluate.

Power. A mother or father who has just lost a spouse, and maybe friends, may feel with desperation the need to feel powerful, to take control of life. Children may be the only people she feels she has control over. A single parent does need to be head of her household—but for the *children's* sake, not for the sake of feeling powerful.

Pride. Your children are experiencing pressures from home, friends, and school. Don't add to their burdens by demanding they become *superkids*. It may make us parents feel great to see that our children get straight *A's*, that they are the best athletes, but is that proud feeling worth the weight of anxiety we may add to our kids?

Punishment. There is a difference between discipline and punishment. The focus of discipline is training. The focus of punishment is pain. Never administer punishment in anger. Don't take your rotten day out on your children.

Checkpoints for Self-Control

Discipline begins at home. Home discipline begins with you. Are you disciplined? Are you in control of yourself? Disciplined parents have a better chance at raising disciplined children. What kind of example do you set for your kids? Do you nag them about all the TV they watch, then stay up watching the late show yourself every night? Are you tough with them about all those tardies on their report cards, but punch in late regularly at work yourself? Behind most disciplined children is at least one disciplined parent.

Galatians 5 lists self-control as a fruit of the Spirit. Don't let yourself off by accepting your own bad habits. "Oh, I'm always running late. That's just the way I am." Or, "You know me—I never could stick to a diet." Christ in you gives you the power to change. His death canceled the power of sin. Nothing is stronger than Christ in you.

What's in a *No?*

How valuable is your *no*? Do any of these conversations ever take place in your home?

Child: I want candy.

Parent: No.

Child: I want candy!

Parent: No. It's too close to dinner.

Child: I *want* candy!

Parent: Now why do you want candy so much?

Child: I want candy.

Parent: Okay, here's half a candy bar. Now let me get dinner.

Child: I WANT CANDY!

Parent: Oh, all right! Have the whole thing. But you still have to eat all your dinner! Do you understand? And I mean it!

Or, how about some version of the following scene?

Child: I want to go to Sarah's for the weekend.

Parent: No, her parents are in Europe.

Child: Oh, please! I really want to go!

Parent: No, it wouldn't be right.

Child: Everybody's going to be there. Sally's mom is letting *her* go. I want to go to Sarah's this weekend!

Parent: No, there are no chaperones.

Child: It's not fair. Daddy would let me go!

Parent: Well, okay, you can go. But there better not be any boys there!

If your *no* has lost its buying power, it's time to beef up the value. The Bible says to let your no be *no* and your yes be *yes*.

Here are the stories from some single parents who triumphed over their hesitancy to say no.

Carmen is a twenty-four-year-old single mom who has been divorced for a year. She gave herself a reasonable goal:

> When Jeremy was fourteen months old, I decided I had the patience to enforce *no* to the TV set controls, a small lamp, and a chair in the family room. I removed every other breakable or tempting item so I wouldn't hear the sound of my voice saying *no* all day long. And I stuck to my guns on the TV and lamp. At least Jeremy learned not to mess with those two things. And he learned that I meant it when I said *no*.

Tim, a forty-year-old single father, lost his wife a year ago. With four teenagers in the house, he had to set up house rules:

> One of our house rules says that if my kids ask me for something once and I say no or maybe, I promise I'll think about it and let them know if I decide we can afford it now or later. But if they nag me about it, or if they try to pressure me into buying what they want, the subject is closed for six months.

Janet is thirty, with her hands full as the single mother of three. She shared this with me:

> I sat at the table with my kids, and we wrote out all the rules and situations we could think of. So they already know 90 percent of

the time what my answer will be and why. I find the more I do in advance of the situation, the better. I can be more objective.

What a difference saying no and sticking to it made in these three families! Trust and relationships improved dramatically as parents and children operated within dependable guidelines.

Pay Attention—to the Child and his Actions

We need to listen to our children and do our best to understand them. Most of us don't have to reach far back into our own lives to remember the frustration of feeling no one understands us, and that the authority figure is acting unreasonably.

Yet we need to pay attention to the child's actions, as well as his motivations. We need to speak to the actions that need to be spoken to. Could the following conversation take place in your home? What's wrong with the exchange?

Child: I want a Coke.

Parent: It's too late for a Coke.

Child: I want some!

Parent: Okay! (Parent pours out a nice glass of Coke.)

Child: No! I don't want it in a glass. I want it in the bottle!

Parent: Uh-oh. (Parent pours Coke back into the bottle.)

Child: This one's yucky! I won't drink it! I want 7-Up.

Parent: Oh, you really are a tired one, aren't you? Better get off to bed.

This parent may be right. The child probably is tired, and that might help to explain the behavior. But the action needs to be disciplined, not excused for reason of fatigue. That behavior needs to change, and it will never change if the parent provides excuses.

Parent: It's your night to do the dishes.

Child: I'm not going to.

Parent: We've agreed to take turns, and it's your turn.

Child: Well, I'm not going to do them.

Parent: Why are you behaving this way?

Child: Daddy doesn't make me do dishes. (Tears.)

Parent: It'll be okay. You miss your daddy, don't you? Go on outside. You don't have to do the dishes today.

Do you let your kids get by with selfish behavior just because you feel sorry for them—poor waifs without a mom or dad? Empathize, understand, but discipline.

She wouldn't act that way if she weren't missing her dad, reasoned the mother in this story. But she neglected to consider how getting away with such behavior affects her daughter. A self-seeking child grows into a self-seeking adult.

In *Parent Power*, Dr. Wright encourages us to treat our child's behavior, no matter what the cause:

Trying to figure out why a child does something, what needs drive him to do a thing, is often a waste of time ... But ignoring the cause and focusing on the behavior does work.

I don't think we should ignore the contributing causes for bad behavior. I think the parent above should sympathize and acknowledge the child's feelings and hurts. But we can't stop there. The behavior needs attention. The discipline needs follow-through. *I know you miss your dad, and I'm sorry (or, and I miss him too sometimes). I understand what you're saying. But the dishes still have to be done, and it's your turn to do them.*

Teamwork

Single-parent families can become efficient teams. Children may learn more responsibility and feel more important to the running of the "team" than children in two-parent families. When my own little family sits down at the dinner table, I can usually count on my eight-year-old to ask, "Well, how was your day, Mom?" That little girl has taught me about teamwork, even in the little things.

As a parent, I need to know my child, what she can do, what would be fair to expect her to do as a member of the team. I expect my eight-year-old to clean her room—that includes everything except vacuuming. I also expect my five-year-old to clean her room. But for her, that means toys in the toy chest, and no clothes on the floor.

One mother discovered her family operated best as a team. On Saturday mornings, Jane and her kids start in the living room and work their way through each room, dividing chores, so the workload isn't too heavy on anyone. When they are all finished, they get to do something fun.

Clarify as much with your teammates as you can before the fact. They should know what the penalty is for failing to fulfill responsibilities. That takes the pressure off of you to decide punishments for offenses. The whole team knows the score—in advance—and can choose whether they want to play by the rules.

Train a Child

Proverbs 22:6 says, "Train a child in the way he should go, and when he is old he will not turn from it." This verse summarizes the two sides of discipline. *Train a child*—training requires a degree of buckling down. It also involves discipline, planning, goal-setting, and follow-through. *In the way he should go*—children aren't the sum of obedience to a set of rules. Each child is different. A good parent knows his child and perceives "the way he should go."

Things to Think About/Discuss

1. What behavior is being rewarded in each of these situations? What options does the parent have? What would you do?

Child: I never get what the other kids get.
Parent: Okay, you can have it.

Child: Mother, Peggy told Ryan to go jump in the lake.
Parent: Peggy, you get in here. You're in big trouble!

Parent: Stop that fighting! Who started it?

Child: I'm just not hungry for peas. Can I have dessert?
Parent: Okay.

Child: Mom, the phone's for you.
Parent: Tell them I'm not home.

2. Over the past month, have you *buckled down* or *backed off* more often? What could you do to restore balance?

3. What usually motivates you when you *back off* (pity, popularity, pooped, planning, other)?

4. What usually motivates you when you *buckle down* (power, pride, punishment, planning, other)?

5. Would you be happy if your children had the same degree of self-discipline and self-control as you have? Why or why not?

14

TO REMARRY OR NOT TO REMARRY (THAT IS THE QUESTION)

Serial marriages have become the trend of the 80's.
We may be fed up with a specific marriage
or with specific marriages,
but we still believe in the institution.
Single Parent, May 1985

WHAT DO CINDERELLA, SNOW White, and Hansel and Gretel have in common? Think about it. Why, even Goldilocks probably had a wicked stepmother. Who else would have allowed her to go out in the woods alone?

Even fairy tales have blended families, but most of today's blended families don't have fairy-tale endings. Serial marriages are on the rise.

Different Strokes for Different Folks

Mary did the best she could to be both mother and father to her four children. Every morning she rose at 5 A.M. to pray, cook a hot breakfast, pack lunches, and look over her notes before the day's presentations.

By 7 A.M., breakfast ready, clothes and books set out for the children, Mary woke each child with a gentle kiss. At eight o'clock she drove the children to school, checked in with each teacher, and with open declarations of love and affection on both sides, bade her children a cheery good morning.

After a hard day at the office, Mary, joyfully reunited with her children, helped each child complete homework before dinner (Mary had a knack for making calculus fun). The kids, as usual, couldn't get enough of Mary's broccoli casserole, fresh baked fish, salad, mashed potatoes, and fresh fruit pie. Dinner was the time when the children could openly discuss problems and triumphs and receive mutual support.

After a family stroll and completion of nightly routines: reading books, a family sing, and prayers, Mary tucked her family safely into bed. Before she drifted off to a sound night's sleep, Mary thought happily, "Why would anyone ever want to remarry?"

Becky had come to the same conclusion—no remarriage for her—but her route differed considerably from Mary's. Becky hated mornings. Her three-year-old woke up (and shared her wakefulness with Mom) at 5:45 A.M. The kid had an interior alarm system. Becky stumbled out of bed and tried to find the Cheerios.

When she finally succeeded in rousing her other three children, it was late. "Hurry up—eat, dress! You'll be late for school again!" shouted Becky.

Somehow Becky got the kids out of the house by 8:20, although she hadn't had time to fix lunches and could barely scrape lunch money together. Her kids hated hot lunch.

The boss yelled at Becky when she came in panting six minutes late. "Only seven hours and fifty-four minutes to go," thought Becky.

After work Becky had to run #1 child to the ballfield, #3 child to ballet lessons, and #4 had a dentist appointment. #2 griped because she never got to do anything. Becky wanted to get fast food for dinner (the kids were already fighting over McDonald's vs. Taco Bell), but those restaurant people would demand cash.

Becky gave in to the kids' plea to eat their TV dinners in front of the TV. It was late, and she was too tired to hear all their complaints about the peas or beans. "It isn't fair," thought Becky. "I have all I can handle, and then some. I can't handle one more responsibility. If I had to cook a real meal or make conversation in the evenings, I'd die. I will never remarry. Anyway, my first husband was a good bet for a faithful, loving husband, and look what he did to me. No way am I going to go through that again!"

Nancy's children had adjusted beautifully to the divorce. Her career had never been better. Nancy had never felt so much in control, so happy. "All I need now," she thought, "is a man."

Dora was lonely. Her car needed repairs, and she hadn't had the oil changed since Fred left. She could never raise these four kids by herself; they needed a father. Dora didn't want to work forty hours a week. She was used to two incomes, family vacations, and having someone to bake for. "I was not meant to stay single," thought Dora. "I need a husband."

These are answers single parents give on the subject of remarriage:

> I can't imagine another adult in our home. I know I'd always end up taking sides with my kids. And that's not the way a marriage is supposed to work.

> I don't want to spend the rest of my life alone. What am I going to do after the kids are grown and gone?

> Right now we're making it as a family. I'm not about to upset that delicate balance by bringing in a whole new set of problems to force more readjustments.
>
> I'll get married again, and probably for the wrong reason: Sex. I'm a Christian and can't allow myself sexual relationships. But I'm a woman and can't stand the thought of never having sex again, either.
>
> How could I bring in a new father? In my bedroom, one wall is covered with drawings and love notes to me from my kids. How at home and romantic would a man feel in that atmosphere—and I could never take down those drawings!
>
> My kids need another parent, and they *want* another parent. So why not expect to get married again?

It's amazing how many attitudes people express about remarriage. The responses above may be more surprising when I tell you that they were all expressed by the same person, on different days over the past year. Or maybe you aren't surprised. Maybe you have felt a similar internal struggle.

The Facts

Listen to these eye-opening statistics: According to *Single Parent Magazine*, 85 percent of divorced people remarry within five years after their decrees are final. Seventy-five percent of remarriages involving children from former marriages fail. Three-fourths of those who divorce twice will remarry a third time (*Marriage and Divorce Today*).

The cold, hard facts look pretty scary, don't they? Trust in the Lord in your decision-making process: "If any of you lacks wisdom, he should ask God, who gives generously to all without finding fault, and it will be given to him" (James 1:5).

Remarriage and You

No one can tell you whether or not remarriage is for you. As you prayerfully consider the question of remarriage, think through the following guidelines.

Am I a whole person now?
Marriage is not the uniting of two halves, but two whole people. Work on being complete and content right now. Then you will have a valuable contribution toward another marriage partnership. You will be free to choose marriage because you love someone, not because you need that person to make you whole.

Don't forget that God is your Husband/Partner right now. You have a whole family already.

Realize that you are loved by God. You are valuable because God loves you and considers you valuable. You don't have to have a new love to feel good about yourself.

Am I desperate?
Age and finances are not good reasons to remarry. So don't let a fear of growing old alone or panic of poverty push you into marrying someone you wouldn't have dated the first time around.

Desperate people have poor perspectives. Don't rush into anything. Give yourself time and distance to gain a healthy perspective.

Am I realistic?
Ah, romance ... Don't let the right man/woman get away because he doesn't look like Tom Selleck or she doesn't look like Vanna White. But just because we're older doesn't mean we're immune

to the blindness that so frequently accompanies romance. I love that romantic stage, when everyone puts his best foot forward. Trouble is, we all have two feet. Wait for the other shoe to fall.

Don't be afraid to hear what other people think about your new love. Although sometimes people can be cruel and unjustly critical and you need to make your own decisions, there is probably more to this new love than you see when you're with him. He has an established life, and you should learn all you can about it.

I was one of those nice girls in high school who always liked the wild boys. "But he is so wonderful, a different person when he's with me," I'd answer my girlfriends' objections. And so he was. But we need to be able to love all of a person, not just the guy who's standing in front of us with his best foot forward.

Am I healed?

If we are not healed, we may marry to stop or ease the hurt. Or we may refuse to marry because the open wound is too tender to let anyone get close to us.

A person who refuses to see her part in the breakup of her marriage may not feel she has a problem. But she needs healing of a different sort. And if she doesn't heal, she may repeat her past mistakes.

So give yourself time to heal.

Am I afraid?

Some of your bitterness, or your ability to find everything wrong with anyone you date, may stem from fear.

The first tactical maneuver for fighting fear is to face it. Admit you're afraid of being hurt again. Tell God. Tell the other person, if appropriate. Stop blaming the shortcomings in other people and the world for your fears.

The Bible says that perfect love casts out fear. Since God is the only one who can offer us perfect love, it makes sense to look to him to help rid ourselves of fear.

Am I selfish?

Marriage should develop from a spirit of giving. Are you considering marriage because you want to give to the person, or because it seems the best solution to your own problems?

It's easy for us to get so set in our ways that we would resent anyone invading our space, our privacy, our domain. I worry about this one and pray that God will keep me soft (not weak) and pliable in a world that seems to demand I grow hard.

Am I prepared?

When families plan to unite, they'd better be prepared. Whether you call them *step-families*, *blended families*, or *reconstituted homes*, these new groupings of individuals will need to work together.

Have you as parents given each other the *permission to parent*? Can he feel free to send your kids to their rooms, or will you resent the interference? Can you force his children to eat their vegetables, or will he side with the kids?

Have you worked it out with the absent parents, the "ex's" to see where they fit in? Have all the children had the opportunity to voice their opinions and fears? Have you and your future spouse been open about your expectations for this marriage? Have you worked out finances, wills, allowances?

Am I committed?

If you enter this new marriage with the idea that the back door is always open if things don't work out, you will very likely be one of the 75 percent whose remarriages don't work out. But if you close the back door and commit yourselves to your new family, asking God daily for help in making this marriage work, you will have a solid foundation of love and belonging.

Things to Think About/Discuss

1. Do you think you will remarry? Why or why not?

2. List five fears you have about getting married again.

3. Now list five fears you have about not getting married again. Ask, "What if this fear were realized?" for each item.

4. Name three current problems you face as a single parent that could make you feel desperate to remarry. What solutions are you working on to face those problems?

5. How far along do you think you've come in the healing process? In what ways are you more *whole* now than when you were married? Be specific.

For more information and ideas you might write to the Stepfamily Association, 28 Allegheny Avenue, Townson, MD 21204; 301/823-7570.

PART IV

NO TEMPTATION HAS SEIZED YOU
EXCEPT WHAT IS COMMON TO MAN.
AND GOD IS FAITHFUL; HE WILL NOT LET YOU
BE TEMPTED
BEYOND WHAT YOU CAN BEAR. BUT WHEN
YOU ARE TEMPTED, HE WILL
ALSO PROVIDE A WAY OUT
SO THAT YOU CAN STAND UP
UNDER IT.

1 Corinthians 10:13

15

CHILD SUPPORT

As a single person, you'd better acquaint yourself with some rather unusual laws that are still on the books:

A little town in Vermont has a law that prohibits any unmarried person from riding an ugly horse to church.

In Wakefield, Rhode Island, it's against the law for an unmarried woman over 200 pounds to ride a horse to church (even if the horse is not ugly).

A small town in Missouri prohibits the hanging of an unmarried woman's lingerie on a backyard clothesline with a single man's shorts.

It's a violation of the law in Columbia, Pennsylvania for any single person to play dominoes, cards, or checkers on Sunday.

> Any unmarried male who is caught fishing in Cobre, Nevada may be fined $25 or a week in the local jail.
>
> And in Beckley, Washington unmarried young women are forbidden to drink coffee on Sunday after 6 P.M.

Actually, I've never run into any questions about these laws. Most of the questions single parents are concerned about deal with child support or visitation rights.

Child Support Laws

Although child support laws vary from state to state, practices are fairly standard because the federal government is concerned with the collection of finances involved. Following are some common questions about child support.

How soon can I be granted child support?
Child support can be required from the moment of separation. You will need to get a child-support order from the court, approved by a judge. Although it is possible to work out a private arrangement, such agreements are hard to enforce. Divorce and separation agreements usually include child-support orders. It's probably best to get a lawyer who specializes in family law.

I've never been married. Can I get child support?
You can receive child support if you are able to establish paternity. One way to do this is through your state's child support enforcement agency, the IV-D program. Contact your local social office or your courthouse.

I don't know where my child's father is. How can I get child support from him?

You can apply for the state parent-locator service. They request information from other states and from the federal parent-locator service. But the process takes a long time. Do all you can to find the noncustodial parent on your own. If you think he or she might live in a certain city, dial directory information (1-area code-555-1212).

I've given up on child support.

It can be very hard to enforce, but child support is just that—support for your child. You owe it to your child to try to get the money he's entitled to. On the other hand, life will be easier if you can manage your finances without depending on child support to pay the bills.

If it's been awhile since you've tried to collect child support, you might try again. New laws have made it easier to enforce child support. Contact your state agency.

How will the child support be collected?

There are several options. The 1985 Child Support Enforcement Amendments require a wage attachment where the money is taken from the paycheck of the absent parent. If the absent parent does not work, or is self-employed, this method may not work.

Some states allow garnishments of unemployment benefits or social security or workman's compensation benefits.

If your state agency has been handling your case and can confirm that the child support due you is over $500, and if you know the absent parent's address and social security number, they may be able to intercept the absent parent's tax refund for state and federal taxes.

If the absent parent lives in another state, you may need to file a Uniform Reciprocal Enforcement of Support Agreement (URESA) so that his or her state will take over the action.

One of the most common methods of collection is to get the absent parent declared in contempt of court; ultimately the punishment would be jail if he or she does not pay. But not all judges will jail nonpaying parents, and it may take many hearings.

Can I keep my ex-husband from seeing the kids if he won't pay child support?

In most states, these issues—child support and visitation—are kept completely separate. If you want a judge to be on your side, don't deny visitation. However, in some states, denial of visitation is a possible defense to nonpayment of support. Again, check with your state agency.

What can I do to receive more child support?

The best divorce decrees contain provisions for regular increases. If yours does not, you will need to get a lawyer and ask for a court hearing for modification of child support. You will need to show increased need and change in circumstances (your own and those of your ex-spouse).

More About Child Support

In 1985, 45.4 percent of female single-parent families lived below the poverty line. The median annual income for all single custodial mothers as of March, 1986 was $9,858. The average amount of child support paid in 1983 was $210 per month. Whatever the child support arrangement, children should not be involved in the mechanics of child support.

Things to Think About/Discuss

1. Are you familiar with child support legislation? Did any of the facts discussed in this chapter surprise you? Which ones? Why?

2. If you are a custodial single parent, do you feel you are receiving adequate child support to cover your children's needs? Why or why not?

3. If you are a parent with visitation rights, do you feel that the child support you pay effectively provides for your children's needs? Why or why not?

4. For more information, contact these resource centers:

Office of Child Support Enforcement
6110 Executive Boulevard, Room 900
Rockville, MD 20852

Handbook on Child Support Enforcement
Handbook, 628 M
Pueblo, CO 81009
(Ask for a free copy of the handbook.)

Single Parent Resource Center
1165 Broadway, Suite 504
New York, NY 10001
212/213-0047

16

WHAT ABOUT VISITATION?

VISITATION. SOUNDS LIKE SOMEthing we do to prisoners on holidays. When my girls' father wants to have the kids visit him over spring break, I don't like it; *I* want to spend that time with them. But when he goes for months without contacting them, I don't like that, either; my kids deserve better attention.

Few divorced people ever feel they have fair visitation. As long as two divorced parents both want time with their kids, visitation will be a source of conflict. Since there is so much potential for misunderstanding between separated or divorced parents, the clearer you both are on the legalities of visitation, the smoother the arrangements should go.

Legal Questions

Visitation is the legal term for arrangements made for the noncustodial parent to see a child. It is the second most hotly-debated topic between divorcing spouses (child support and other financial arrangements usually hold first place). Many times in the visitation struggle, children become pawns for two warring parents. In this chapter we'll take a look at some questions parents ask about visitation.

What visitation terms can I expect?

If you don't request specific terms of visitation in a divorce or separation decree, the judge will probably include "reasonable visitation" or "reasonable and seasonable visitation" in your court order. But most divorce lawyers warn the noncustodial parent against accepting these general terms. "Reasonable" visitation is almost impossible to enforce. What seems "reasonable" to one parent may not seem so to the other.

The most common specified visitation terms arrange for weekend visits twice a month, and a period of time during summer vacation. Some parents arrange for time during the week. It's also recommended that you specify holiday arrangements: Name the holidays to be alternated according to even and odd years.

What can I do to get my "reasonable and seasonable" visitation spelled out?

To change the terms of your decree or court order, most states require that you prove a "change of circumstances" so that the court can reopen your case. You'll need an attorney. Also, you may need to prove that your ex-spouse has violated your reasonable visitation clause.

Now that my ex-husband has moved to another state, who should pay for sending the kids to see me?

Child support cannot be viewed as transportation money; it's a separate issue. You can talk to the other parent and try to work out a shared expense agreement, but legally you can't force the custodial parent to pay for transportation, unless there is provision in the court order.

Since my wife moved to another state, she won't let the kids come back to visit me. How can I enforce my visitation rights?

This is one of the hardest situations because there is no agreement between states that allows you to file a court action where you live that can be transferred to another state. If you can hire an attorney in the other state, you can ask courts there to enforce your court order from the state where it was issued, under provisions of the Uniform Child Custody Jurisdiction Act (UCCJA) and Parental Kidnapping Prevention Action.

My ex-spouse is a bad influence on the kids. Or, my ex-spouse claims I am a bad influence on my kids.

Both you and your ex-spouse should hire attorneys if such a dispute arises. "Bad influence" is not enough to eliminate visitation rights. Ask a lawyer to see what evidence would be required to deny visitation in your state. If the claim is unfounded, it will probably be withdrawn before you reach court. If the dispute goes to court, each side must produce evidence.

It's possible that visitation arrangements might be made to work around the problem: no overnight visits if the noncustodial parent is living with a boyfriend or girlfriend, supervised visitation if there has been a problem with drugs or alcohol.

What can I do if I'm denied visitation?

If you can prove that the custodial parent has disobeyed the court order, she could be found in contempt of court. For your petition in court you must supply evidence: a calendar specifically noting dates and times of requests for visitation and denials, letters, etc.

You might try having a lawyer write a letter for you to the custodial parent, informing your ex-spouse of your decision to go to court if visitation agreements are not complied with.

One thing you cannot do is withhold child support from the custodial parent. In most states the issues of visitation and child support are distinct.

What can I do to locate my ex-spouse and kids?
You can use the Federal Parent Locator Service to locate a parent and child to enforce visitation orders, according to the federal Parental Kidnapping Prevention Act. The provision is included in 42 U.S.C. Sec. 663.

For the Kids' Sake

Parents, please do what is best for your kids! It's a sad statement on Christian conduct when Christian parents have to turn their problems over to the courts. Paul wrote to the Corinthians, shaming them for not being able to handle their problems out of court. Try to separate your anger from your kids' needs. Many horrible husbands and wives turn out to be good fathers and mothers.

Custodial parents, in the long run your children will probably be better adjusted if they have access to both parents, if they maintain healthy relationships with both parents. Over 35 percent of children living with their moms have no contact with their fathers. And three out of four fathers don't see their children as often as they are permitted in their visitation agreements. If your child's other parent wants to see your child, your child is probably lucky.

Noncustodial parents, if you are not regularly visiting your child, analyze the reasons for your neglect. If you are visiting your children and would like to have more time, you'll have a better chance of getting more time if you try to fit in with plans made by your child and the custodial parent. It's hard for children to be split into two homes, continually having to make choices between parents, friends, and activities. Try to understand and fit in.

Visitation is hard enough already; don't make it any harder on you or the kids.

Things to Think About/Discuss

1. Do you or does your ex-spouse have "reasonable" and/or "seasonable" visitation of your children? Do you feel the arrangement works? Why or why not?

2. Do you think your children feel like pawns between you and your ex-spouse? Write down your thoughts. Then ask your children. Be prepared for their honesty.

3. How do you feel about your ex-spouse's influence on your children? Is this attitude helpful or harmful to your children? Why?

4. Whether you are a custodial or noncustodial parent, do you separate any feelings toward your spouse from your children's needs? Where do you need to improve?

17

MANIPULATION—A GAME?

All children soon acquire the art of parent manipulation, playing one parent against the other. It's called child power! Children of divorce usually become Manipulation Masters. Are any of these games being played at your house?

The Love Game: "If you really loved me ... you'd let me stay up later ... you'd let me go out with my friends ... you wouldn't make me do that."

The Guilt Game: "I just miss my Mommy and want to stay up late with you." Or, "If Daddy were still here ... I'd have somebody to play with ... we could afford to eat out."

The Threat Game: "Okay, I'll just go live with Daddy." Or, "I don't like it here. Mommy lets us stay up." And, "Daddy never makes me eat lima beans."

Parent Vs. Parent

Morals and values

What if a single parent feels the child's other parent may undermine his moral training and give him different values? Sometimes the things a parent hears when the kids come back from a visit with the noncustodial parent make the custodial parent wonder if the training the kids receive during the week is being undone over the weekend.

Here's what some single parents advise:

> Don't underestimate your children, especially if they know Christ. I was afraid my kids would see their father was sleeping with different women and then decide it would be okay for them, too. We talked about it. They accept their father for who he is, but my kids have their own morals based on the Scriptures.

> Pray for your children. I felt I had to tell my children that they needed to form their own values, even if theirs differed from their mother's. But I was careful not to run down their mother. I just prayed they'd remember right from wrong.

> You have to trust your kids, and you have to trust God at work in them.

Competition

Other custodial parents feel threatened because the children have such unusual, out-of-the-ordinary experiences during their short visits with the other parent. Peanut butter and jelly sandwiches, laundry, and the car pool don't seem to compete with steak or pizza, weekends at Disneyland, or an annual ski trip.

But listen to one noncustodial father's self defense:

> Look, I only see my kids about once a month. I don't want to spend those few days in my little apartment. I want them to have a good time. Why shouldn't I buy them gifts? I can afford it, and what better way could I spend the money?

Pettiness and competition for the affections of the children hurt everyone involved. But noncustodial parents should realize that their children need to see them and get to know them in natural settings. And the kids can't do that if the parent keeps them so busy there's no time to talk. So let them see you in your daily life. Let them have a real life when they are with you, a real life with a real parent.

Here's two single parents' advice from both sides of the issue:

> My children's father takes the kids on vacations, and I'm lucky if I can afford a walk to the grocery store. But you can't be competitive. Even if you come out on top, the kids lose. All you can do is be the best parent you can be and do what you know is right. Kids may be temporarily blinded by Disneyland, but they will regain their sight.

> I'm a reformed Disneyland-Dad. I finally ran out of places to take my son, and we went back to being father and son, instead of just pals. He didn't like it at first, but it's worked out better.

Kids in the middle

Sometimes children use the option of going to live with the other parent as a threat or manipulation technique. Listen in on this conversation between three single parents as they discuss responses:

Mike: When Sarah says, "Then I'll go live with Mom," I say, "That's fine. I'll help you pack your bags." That usually puts an end to the threat.

Tammy: I think that's the worst way to handle her threat. I told my daughter that I would be very hurt if she moved out, that I was as committed to her as her father is and didn't want her to leave. That's how I felt, and that's what I said. I don't believe in answering a threat with a threat.

Carrie: I agree that you should offer to help her pack and move. But you need to be prepared to follow through with your offer because he or she just might take you up on it. My son did. He lived for nine months with his dad, and then he asked to come home. Letting him go was the right thing to do. He never would have believed me if I had tried to tell him he wouldn't be happy with his father.

Tammy: Well, I don't want to let my daughter go, and I'll do whatever I can to prevent it.

Carrie: But you can't prevent it forever. We all have to be willing to let a child make his own decisions when he is old enough. That's part of parenting, letting our children be free to fail and to make mistakes. The father of the prodigal son was wise enough to know when to let go. He paid a great price, but he got his son back. What would have happened if he had refused to let his son go?

Maybe you agree with one of the three single parents in this conversation. Or else, depending on your mood, your opinion goes back and forth with theirs. But as parents we must be careful not to let our kids use the manipulation game on us. It won't improve our relationship with them—or with the other parent. Don't let threats throw you into a vicious cycle.

Tips for Noncustodial Parents

As a noncustodial parent, you play a difficult role. Maybe you miss your kids desperately and can't believe *she* got custody (after all she's done). Or maybe you feel guilty because you really don't want to see your kids—it brings back so many awful memories of your failed marriage. But even though you don't see your children as much as the other parent, you still need to exercise your parenting skills. And one of your most important jobs is to develop trust and honesty. Here are a few tips on how to keep a good relationship with your kids.

Keep your promises. If there is even a chance that you can't follow through on a promise, don't make the promise. Your kids need to know that your word is good.

Be an encourager. Although you're not with them for morning oatmeal, afterschool chores, and bedtime stories, and you can't make it to every recital or ballgame, you *can* be an encourager. Let them know you're their #1 fan.

Don't take everything personally. As your kids grow older, their friends will become increasingly important to them. Your kids may not want to spend time with you because they might miss out on school activities or fun with friends. That doesn't mean they want you out of their lives. You may just need to work harder at adjusting to their needs and fitting in.

Ask for your own copies of the children's school records and report cards. Make your own appointments to meet with their teachers.

Be regular and punctual on visitations, when you pick them up and drop them off. Your consistency and attention demonstrate to your kids that you think your time with them is valuable.

Don't criticize the custodial parent in front of the children. It won't make you look "better" than the other parent, and it will make your children uncomfortable, giving them the feeling that they have to take "sides."

Don't be afraid to parent. Be a parent, not a type of grandparent.

Tips for Custodial Parents

As a custodial parent, you may feel that your kids think life with you is drab and dull compared to their exciting weekends. But don't let the "doldrums" set into your relationship with your kids. Make sure that you always have open ears and an open heart for your children. Here are some suggestions:

Let your children feel free to tell you about the great time they had at their other parent's. But don't pump the kids for information about the other parent.

Keep them out of child-support disputes. Don't develop the habit of using the kids as messengers to relay your feelings or information to your ex-spouse.

Try to help your children remember to schedule their special activities with friends on weekends that won't interfere with visitation.

Don't criticize or belittle the absent parent. Your children need all the benefits they can receive from both parents. You can help them focus on the positive characteristics of that parent.

Both parents need to work hard at keeping the focus on the children and not on themselves. If you can't work together, side by side, at least try to work in parallel lines. You may have stopped being husband and wife, but you can't stop being father and mother.

Things to Think About/Discuss

1. Are your kids Manipulation Monsters? Which of the games do they play (Love, Guilt, Threat)? How?

2. If you are a custodial parent, do you feel threatened by your ex-spouse and his time with your kids? In what ways? What can you do about it?

3. If you are a noncustodial parent, what can you do to make your time with your children *real*?

4. What steps can you take to help your children develop strong moral values and also improve your relationship with them?

18

EMOTIONS AND KIDS

The chief trouble with children
is that they are human.

THIS SAYING IS A GOOD REMINDER for me whenever I get exasperated with my kids. It's easy to forget that, like me, my kids are only too human. They have a broad range of emotions that add depth to their personalities and makes them who they are. If we want to help our children adjust to a single-parent family, we must understand what they are feeling. That's not always easy. Because I'm an adult and they are children, sometimes it's hard for me to reach back into my past to remember what it felt like to be a kid.

Children run the gamut of emotions—one right after the other. Their cycles of grief and recovery are usually harder to track than the adult grief cycle. But most of the common responses of children who have just lost a parent through death or divorce can fit into one of four categories: fear, anger, loss of self-esteem, and depression. Of course, many other responses are possible, and these emotions may show themselves in other ways.

Fear

A child who has lost one parent may logically fear she is in danger of losing her other parent. This fear in a young child may make her cling to her parent and fuss whenever she is left behind. A teenager may withdraw from the custodial parent, protecting himself against the possibility that that parent may leave, too.

A regression in development might be an indicator of fear or anxiety: things such as bed-wetting, failing classwork, babytalk from a six-year-old. Older children may develop nervous habits such as biting their fingernails or crying hysterically when disappointed.

Fear can manifest itself as worry. A seven-year-old may be needlessly anxious about his mother's health. An eleven-year-old might worry excessively about family finances.

What can I do?

What can you do for your children when you recognize their fears? Start by letting them talk about their fears. Let them know you're trying to understand. When you can legitimately reason away certain fears, do it. For example, assure them that you have no intention of leaving. Tell them you've had a medical exam and are in good shape. Explain that if something ever happened to you, they wouldn't be left alone—Grandma and Gramps, or Auntie and Uncle would care for them. Explain that just because you may not have enough money for them to go to the movies, you have enough to pay the rent and put groceries on the table.

But you need to be honest. Your children have to be able to trust you. Don't tell them there's no danger that you might lose your house if that danger actually exists.

You need to be able to point them to God for their ultimate security. And to do that, you will have to look to God yourself. Your children will catch your fears and anxieties; they can sense your worry. Trust Christ to help you as you try to regain order in your single-parent family. Even when you admit to your kids that you're frightened about the unknown, too, explain that in your heart you know (even if at the moment you don't feel it) that God is in control and still has a wonderful plan for all of you. He does!

Single parents have to walk the fine line between pretending everything is rosy, and dumping adult fears on children. Somewhere in-between those extremes is the best, most responsible path. Pray that God will give you the right words and that he will protect your children when you say the wrong things. Above all, pray with your kids. Learn to trust God together as a family.

Anger

These are some of the verbal messages that can give parents the red alert that their children are angry:

I won't—and you can't make me!

I'll go if I want to—there's nothing you can do to stop me!

Get away! I don't want you!

I don't care if it *is* Dad's weekend—I won't go with him.

I'm not going to bed!

Ever heard words like these from your children? Parents with angry children become frustrated and often speak like this:

I don't know what to do. Ted's turned into a bully at school.

Marty never used to get in fights. He was always a good kid.

> Mandy is so mean to her little brother and sister, I'm afraid she's really going to hurt them.
>
> Susan is a big grouch. Nothing pleases her—especially me!
>
> Jason is so irritable and touchy, I can hardly stand to be in the same house with him.
>
> What can I do with Jan? She is defiant. I tell her she can't go out with her friends. She looks me straight in the eyes and then walks out. I never know where she is or when (or if) she will come home.
>
> I'm really worried about Bonnie. She sits in her room by herself, and she hardly ever talks to me.

Anger comes in many different shapes. Keep in mind that all children (and all adults) get angry. We don't want to blame all of our problems on the fact that we're single parents. But a sudden change in behavior or an enduring anger may be related to the divorce or death in the family.

What can I do?

I'm not a psychiatrist. And, as I suggest at the end of this chapter, you should seek professional help if you feel your child's problems are serious. All I can offer is my own experience and the experiences of other single parents.

Mary Ann, a thirty-four-year-old single homemaker, shared her story:

> My daughter Sarah became rude and disobedient after her father moved out. She would say anything to hurt my feelings: "I hate you!" Or, "I don't have anything to say!" And, "Daddy

> probably left you because you're so ugly or so stupid."
>
> I tried every kind of discipline, but nothing affected her. Finally I told her I loved her, and then I left her alone. I tried not to defend myself or react to her anger. And slowly her anger subsided, and she came back to me. I think we're closer now than we've ever been. She knows that her anger can't stop me from loving her.

Jim is a businessman and single father of two. He relates what happened when his wife left:

> I knew how angry my sons were that their mother had left. At first I tried to distract them or talk them out of being angry. I think I was trying the same thing with myself. We were getting nowhere. Then I was honest with them. I told them that, frankly, I was angry with their mother, too. She was probably angry with me. But I didn't want to hold onto my anger, and I didn't want them to have to hang onto theirs forever either. So we decided to pray that God would help us get over our anger and get on with our lives.

Ann admitted, "My oldest daughter mirrors all my emotions. My only hope of helping her get over her anger and hostility toward her father is for me to get over mine. I'm trying."

Randy's son Andrew constantly lashed out at his father and his absent mother, and Randy let him. This is why:

> I know that Andrew's anger is protecting him from being sad. For right now, I'm going to let him be angry. I don't think he can handle the hurt yet—somehow anger is easier.

All of these parents recognized that feeling angry was a natural response for their chidlren. They tried not to take personally what their children said. Instead, they realized that part of grief is the anger phase and that anger, too, is part of the healing process.

Like these parents, we need to give our children space and time to be themselves—and to be honest with themselves and us.

Dr. Archibald D. Hart writes:

> Every child should, therefore, be allowed the freedom to feel angry, and be shown ways to express that anger without hurting others. Denying the child this freedom will only cause him or her to suppress the anger. There is then a greater risk that the child will use passive and indirect ways of expressing anger; this is always less healthy than being allowed to feel and express anger indirectly (p. 104).

Dr. Hart promotes a freedom of expression for children. Children need to know that they are loved whether they are happy or angry. And yet we shouldn't take this to be a green light for permissive parenting. Swihart and Brigham talk about expression within limits:

> Bullies need "tough love." They need to be able to deal with their anger and alter their perception of the world. This means consistent interactions with someone who can set limits, help create a more positive world and yet be open to helping them deal with anger (*Helping Children of Divorce*, Downers Grove, IL: InterVarsity Press, 1982, p. 46).

If we as parents can allow our children free expression of their feelings, we will promote a new openness in our relationships with them. And if we also set some limits to their expression, we teach them about self-control lovingly. It is this type of child who adjusts and feels secure in the world you help him build.

Low Self-Esteem

A child's mother leaves home, or his father moves out. This child may begin to feel that he isn't worth very much. After all, if he were important and valuable, why was his parent so willing to leave him behind? His loss of *self-esteem* may turn him into a hermit, a show-off, or a little grown-up. Let's take a look at the type of kids low self-esteem breeds:

Hermits: Six-to-ten-year-olds frequently show a sense of deep sadness after a divorce or death in the family. They may go off by themselves during school recess or at home. They might not want to be around other kids. They may seem lost in thought, have trouble concentrating, or cry quietly for no apparent reason.

Show-offs: Show-offs seem to exude self-confidence, when they are actually trying to get approval and attention. They may become disruptive at school or do dangerous things. They may simply try to be the best—the best student, the best baseball player, the best acrobat—in order to feel good about themselves.

Little grown-ups: Most children in single-parent families will end up with more responsibilities in the home because now there is more work to do. This can be a healthy step in growing to adulthood. Many children from single-parent homes are far more responsible than their peers. But we need to be careful that our children don't skip childhood. Kids need to be kids. The son who suddenly becomes the "man of the house" and the daughter who turns into a "second mother" may one day resent those lost years of childhood.

What can I do?

How can you build your children's self esteem? Once again, the place to begin is with yourself. You'll need to work on personal self-esteem first. If you can't accept the fact that God loves you and considers you special, you won't sound very convincing when you tell your children that they are valuable and wonderful because God loves them and has made them special.

Even though you may be busier than you've ever been, try to take some time out with your child when you give him your full attention. Look for anything positive you can praise.

You can build a type of confidence in young children by telling them they are the best. Self-esteem may soar—until they begin to get feedback from other sources, peers, and teachers. Then that child may have more trouble trying to feel good about himself. His foundation will have crumbled.

It's vital to build self-esteem on the truth, not on lies. As tempting as it is to say, "Yes, you really are the best artist in the first grade," it's probably more truthful to say, "I love your artwork. Yours will always be the best to me because I love you."

Depression

All of these symptoms we have discussed overlap. The child with low self-esteem will probably also experience depression. And an angry child may very well be afraid.

It would be surprising if a child did not go through some kind of depression after the loss of a parent. Before a divorce, the emotional tension in the home may have contributed to the child's depression. The grief of losing a parent involves depression.

What are some of the warning signs of depression? Young children may whine, cry, and throw tantrums. A child may appear irritable, sad, or bored. He may express guilt feelings, or belittle himself, expressing a fear or expectation of failure. Sometimes a child will suffer physical discomfort such as a headache or an upset stomach. Another child may seem frustrated, and have a short attention span. Sometimes a child will blame others for everything, complaining that he's always left out, nobody plays with him, everybody picks on him, or nobody cares. Sometimes he may overeat or not eat much at all. Or he may become obsessed with studies, sports, or members of the opposite sex. Depression takes many forms.

What can I do?

Try to show your child that you understand his struggles and that he has a right to feel the way he does. Communicate that you love him and accept him even when he feels lousy.

I made the mistake of trying to talk my daughter out of feeling sad. "C'mon, you should be happy!" I said. "You have a mom who loves you, lots of friends, a cute baby sister who thinks you're the greatest! Stop moping around." Or, "Don't cry. You're just tired, and it's late." It didn't work.

It's true there's a time to say, "Come on, let's shake it off and do something fun." Distraction can be a valuable temporary tool. Fun can be good medicine. But kids feel deeply, and it's frustrating to have adults think they can talk you out of the hurt. Children need to know that it's okay for them to feel sad. They shouldn't have to worry about hurting your feelings or making you uncomfortable. They need to know that you love them—even when they are depressed.

If depression persists in your child, or if you feel incapable of helping your child, you may need to seek professional help.

But the help most children need is a wise, understanding, patient parent who will listen to them—whether they are afraid, angry, depressed, or suffering because of a lack of self-esteem. The relationship built on unconditional love and acceptance will impact their lives forever.

Things to Think About/Discuss

1. When are your children most emotional? Why is that?

2. Can you see a grief response in one or more of your children? Which one (fear, anger, loss of self-esteem, depression)?

3. Write down some ways in which you can help your children to express constructively how they are feeling. Then try one of them out with your children this week.

4. What about you? Do you pretend everything is rosy all the time? Or do you dump your anger and fear on your kids? What can you do to strike a healthy balance for yourself?

19

RAISING OKAY KIDS & OTHER CONCERNS

THROUGHOUT THIS BOOK WE have discussed a broad range of questions about single parenting. But the questions don't end here for single parents. We discover new ones every day. Sometimes I wish I had all the answers (other times I'd be happy if I could come up with just one). As Jenny and Katy grow physically, mentally, and spiritually, so do their questions. And so do mine.

This chapter is a hodge-podge of questions and information from my own life and those of single parents I know. I hope you'll find it helpful in your own search for knowledge about how to be the best single parent you can be.

Children of All Ages

Do you ever feel as if you're the only single parent in the world with three preschool-aged children? Don't feel alone. According to the Bureau of the Census, this is how the ages break down for children in single-parent families:

15 percent are under age 3
17 percent are between the ages of 3 and 5
21 percent are between the ages of 6 and 9
29 percent are between the ages of 10 and 14
18 percent are between the ages of 15 and 17

Daycare

Most single parents with young children struggle with the problem of finding adequate daycare (unless you are lucky enough to have accommodating family members nearby). It's very hard to leave kids for the first time, hard to find the right childcare facility.

A good way to find a suitable daycare center is to ask satisfied parents where they have placed their children. But don't go on the recommendation of only one parent. Ask around.

Know your own needs and the personal preferences of your children. Ask your pastor or a local church for helpful information. There are local referral agencies in many areas. You can find the agency closest to you by contacting the National Association for the Education of Young Children at 1-800-424-2460. Decide whether you are looking for a playschool or a more structured setting. Then pick out several and visit them.

Visit a daycare center at least three times, at different hours of the day, before you settle on one facility. Make sure it is licensed by the state. Check with the Better Business Bureau to see if the center has ever had complaints filed against it.

Ask the daycare center for three references from parents of children in the center. When you check with these references, talk long enough to find out if the needs of their children are similar to the needs of your own children.

During your visits, check out the bathrooms and the food areas for cleanliness. Are the kids having fun and relaxing? Are the toys safe and in good shape? Is there enough room to play outside and inside? How do the teachers handle conflicts between children?

It may help to arrive armed with a list of questions for the daycare owner. Here are some ideas:

1. What is the child-to-caregiver ratio? Four or five four-year-olds to one caregiver is good. 8 to 1 is normal. 12 to 1 is too many!
2. How are you licensed?
3. What are the minimum qualifications for caregivers?
4. What kind of turnover is there among caregivers?
5. How much does it cost?
6. What kind of discipline do you employ?
7. What is your curriculum?
8. Do children take a rest in the morning or afternoon?
9. What is the procedure in emergencies?
10. What is the policy concerning sick children?
11. Is the center open during holidays? When the public schools are not in session?

Don't be afraid to ask questions! You are the employer, and this is an important decision.

Mothers and Sons

One single mom expressed this fear: "I can't play baseball or football. I'm afraid my son will grow up to be a Mama's Boy." Her concern is legitimate. Boys with absent fathers have less exposure to their primary role model for masculinity.

Relax! There are ways to help your son identify with his father and the other men in his life. And your problem may not be as unique as it seems. Listen to the remarks of these single moms on this subject:

> I drove my son and myself crazy trying to be mother and father to him. Finally I admitted I had all I could handle just being Mom. I figured life for my son wasn't so different from the lives of his friends whose fathers worked so much they never spent time with their sons anyway.

> I discovered I was forcing my son into a macho image because I was afraid he would turn out gay living with only his mother. The poor kid just didn't like sports. Finally I accepted him as he is and decided not to worry about it. Who says boys have to love sports?

Mothers can facilitate the relationship between their sons and the absent fathers by talking frequently and positively (always truthfully) about the fathers and by encouraging both fathers and sons to interact as much as possible.

Maria was deeply concerned about her son's missing role model:

> It was my concern for a male role model for my son that made me begin to encourage his father to take a more active role in our son's life. I know I can't get in the middle of their relationship, but I can make it easier for them to get together.

Maria looked past her own feelings toward her ex-husband and was willing to help keep her son's and ex-spouse's relationship growing.

Annette had to look deeply into her own emotions first in order to help her sons:

> I think the best thing we single mothers can do for our sons is to get rid of our anger toward their fathers. Boys see themselves as extensions of their dads. If we are bitter and critical about their fathers, how will our sons feel about themselves?

There are other men in your family's world that can provide strong models for masculinity. These mothers may have come up with ideas you haven't yet considered:

> I think the best thing you can do for your son is to reclaim your extended family. Try to see the grandparents, uncles, cousins, etc. more often.

> I felt my son needed male role models, so I prayed about it and asked a single man in our church if he might take the kids out sometimes, work on batting with them, go to a ballgame (at my expense), or just go out for a hotdog. I offered to do the same for his daughter. It's worked out pretty well.

> I felt I really needed a dad-type for my thirteen-year-old son, so I went to the Big Brothers' organization in my city and requested a big brother. I know you have to be really careful today. There are a lot of crazy people in the world—like men who abuse young boys. But my son's big brother was exactly what I was looking for.

> I made the mistake of encouraging my kids to become attached to the first man I started dating after my divorce. When I stopped dating him, the kids were crushed. So I scrambled to

> find another guy and went through the whole thing again. I think we need to look for male friendships for our sons, but those friends shouldn't necessarily be men we date.

And who knows? A boy, especially if he's an older child, may just take care of the problem without Mom's help! Trish's son did:

> My son didn't need a stand-in father; he needed a stand-back mother! When I stopped being so overprotective and let him choose his own friends and activities, my son found his own role models: a coach at school, his friend's father, the youth director at church.

That son's accomplishments should teach us a lot about how to be stand-back single parents who give our kids room to make their own choices.

Teenagers

One day you watch your child come sailing in and out of your kitchen, banging the door behind him. Suddenly you think, "Who was that? Can that almost-grown-up, wild-animal-like creature be *my child*?"

Here's what some clever minds think about those terrible teen years.

> Man is probably the only animal which even attempts to have anything to do with its half-grown young. *George Ross Wells, turn-of-the-century American writer*

> There's nothing wrong with teenagers that reasoning with them won't aggravate. *Unknown*

Never lend your car to anyone to whom you have given birth. *Erma Bombeck*

The trouble with the 1980's as compared to the 1970's is that teenagers no longer rebel and leave home. *Marion Smith*

So what can you do with your teenager? My own kids are not yet teenagers, so I won't presume to give advice. But you'll benefit from (and smile over) these words of advice and encouragement from parents who do have teens:

Get call-waiting!

Kids have to break from their parents sometime. To become independent, they need to struggle—and that struggle is usually with their parents. To establish their own identities, they have to reject their identities as extensions of Mom and Dad.

Get a healthy perspective on your kid's life. Talk with other parents—misery loves company! Somehow it helps to learn that all parents of teens at times fear their kids are headed for juvenile delinquency.

Remember: They can't be teenagers forever. Hang in there!

The typical teenager passes through some regular stages of attitude development. Don't be afraid to call a phase *a phase*.

About junior high age, kids usually develop a *negative attitude*; they become restless, critical, and bored. They are often *rebellious*. Everything seems unfair to them—especially their parents. A child may begin to buck the system he has accepted for so many years.

This mom made it through the rebellious years—take her advice.

> Don't take it personally! When your teen tells you you're the worst mother in the world, that he hates you, that you embarrass him in front of his friends, don't take it personally. Nothing is harder to carry off, but nothing is really more important than your response to his rebellion. He is rebelling at the *system*, not at *you*.

Experimentation is a dangerous element of the teen years. The teen is ready to try new things. Pay close attention during this stage for signs of alcohol or drug abuse. Don't be afraid to ask questions of your teen and his friends.

A Word of Caution

As parents, we need to be on the alert. Over 2,000 teens commit suicide each year in the United States. We need to be able to recognize warning signs of this epidemic teen problem. Some are: loss of appetite, sleep disturbance, loss of enthusiasm about life, interest in the subject of death, withdrawal from friends, self-medication for depression involving drugs and alcohol, mention of suicide, or sudden changes in schoolwork. If you are concerned, don't hesitate to ask your teen direct questions. Also, seek professional help.

The Independence Years

All teens crave *independence*. A teenage girl wants to be her own person, decide what she wants to do, and be responsible for her own life. She may not be as rebellious as before, but she resents interference from her parents. A boy may be embarrassed about having to call his mom to ask permission to go out with the guys.

Here's what one experienced mom says about those difficult years:

> The worst thing a single parent can do is reject a teenager during those difficult years. Believe me, I was tempted! But my daughter was trying to "find herself." She was vulnerable, even though she didn't act like it. And even though she acted as if she wanted me out of her life completely, it would have destroyed her emerging self-concept if her only parent had rejected her.

Hopefully, someday you and your teens will reach the stage of *reconciliation.* Then you can build a new working relationship based on respect and *mutual* acceptance.

Parent Talk

I've found that single parents who have made it through their children's teen years are a great resource of help for me. Let's hear what they have to say on some important aspects of parent and teen interaction. Their responses fall into three categories: respecting privacy and friends, maintaining discipline, and keeping communication lines open.

Respect their choices and friends.
For a year, Mark struggled with his two teenage sons who were constantly at each other's throats. Then he implemented this philosophy for home life:

> The more freedom and responsibility you can give a teenager, the less he will have to fight you for. Let him have a vote, a say,

in what you do as a family. Try to work together to set curfews and consequences for breaking rules, to settle division of labor at home, etc.

After three years of being single, Angie realized she was lonely. Her daughter had grown up and didn't need her mother as much. Still, Angie was concerned about the quality of her daughter's friends. Then she figured out that one day's best friend turned out to be tomorrow's enemy. Here's what Angie learned:

> Be careful with your teenager's friends. Usually kids choose these years to switch from home to peers. Try not to make it you vs. the friends. If you're feeling left out and want to keep your daughter home with you more, she may resent you as an obstacle to her plans. You may not have a lot of say in your teen's choice of friends. But try to remember that there is a high turnover in teen friends. If you don't like a particular buddy, chances are he won't be around forever, anyway.

Maintain discipline

Steve felt strongly that his kids should grow up responsible. Here's his advice:

> Let your teens be teens, but don't stop being a parent. If you have set a reasonable curfew and it's violated, you have to follow through on the consequences. You're still head of the household. And part of your responsibility before God is teaching your children respect.

Kim decided that she needed to prioritize her parental objections:

> Save your objections for things that count! It's not going to destroy your child's moral development if he has a hairstyle you

don't like or bizarre clothes. Decide what's non-negotiable (sex before marriage, drugs, drinking, etc.) and use your parental powers and veto on those things.

Keep the communication lines open

These two moms focus on communication with their teens:

> It might be time now to talk more about a past divorce. A teenager who has never blamed herself for her parents' break-up may now decide it was all her fault. Even though Mom and Dad have been divorced for years, all of a sudden the divorce seems embarrassing.
>
> Be open about sexuality with your teens. Try to keep those communications lines open.

These three dads have formed a network of support for each other. They meet together weekly for encouragement and discuss their relationships with their teens. Here are some of their tips:

> I try to be an unconditional fan of my teenager. I don't approve of everything he does, but I try to find something to approve. I just communicate that I think he's the greatest.
>
> Rack your brain and remember what it was like to be a teen. It's hard to identify with our teenagers. They seem to get upset about insignificant things.
>
> It takes two to make a fight. If you're constantly fighting, you are part of the conflict. It only takes one to stop a fight. You may not be able to keep your teenager from arguing with you, but you can keep it from being a fight. Remember, you're the grown-up.

So teenagers are a crazy adult-kid mix. No wonder it takes work on both sides to maintain a strong parent-teen relationship.

As a parent, you can find ways to give your child positive experiences with responsibility. Write out a plan to increase responsibility and independence in your teen. Leave certain decisions and family duties to him. Above all, let him be free to fail at his tasks and still get another chance.

Remember—even in the tough times together, your children are a gift from the Lord. You must trust the Giver with his gift. He's at work on those gifts, perfecting them and developing them. He can build your single-parent family into a home. And with God as the head of your home, you will always have this reassurance:

> All your sons will be taught by the Lord,
> And great will be your children's peace.
> *Isaiah 54:13*

Things to Think About/Discuss

1. If you are a single mom, are you afraid your son will grow up a Mama's Boy? If you are a single dad, do you worry about raising your daughter without a woman's influence? Why?

2. Make a list of people of the opposite sex you feel comfortable with and who could spend time with your children. Then ask one of them to do something with your child sometime this month.

3. What's your relationship with your teenager like? Do you respect his privacy and friends and maintain discipline?

4. How can you keep the communication lines open with your children? Jot down some ideas. Then share your ideas with your kids.

Resource Organizations for Single Parents

With grateful acknowledgment to Parents Without Partners, *8807 Colesville Road, Silver Spring, MD 20910. Used by permission.*

Big Brothers and Big Sisters of America, 230 North 13th St., Philadelphia, PA 19107, 215/567-2748. The national headquarters maintains lists of local agencies working with children from single-parent homes.

Coalition of State and Local Child Support Enforcement Organizations, c/o Parents Without Partners, Suite 100, 7910 Woodmont Ave., Bethesda, MD 20814, 800/638-8078 or 301/654-8850. Request a list of mutual support organizations working on child support enforcement at state and local levels.

Child Victims of Sexual Abuse Hotline, 800/422-4453. This hotline provides information twenty-four hours a day, seven days a week, for both victims and parents.

Crittenton Services, Child Welfare League of America, 440 1st St., NW, Washington, DC 20001, 202/638-2952. The service provides information and referral for young parents, never-married mothers, and others.

Fatherhood Project, Bank Street College of Education, 610 W. 112th St., New York, NY 10025, 212/663-7200, ext. 246. The project refers single fathers to programs and other resources nationwide and provides information regarding development of new options for male involvement in childrearing.

Family Resource Coalition, 236 N. Michigan Ave., Suite 1625, Chicago, IL 60601, 312/726-4750. The Coalition functions as a clearinghouse for family resource programs throughout the United States and Canada.

Home and School Institute, Special Projects Office, 1201 16th St., NW, Washington, DC 20036, 202/466-3633. The programs and publications available are aimed at helping parents help their children learn at home.

Military Family Support Center, 6501 Loisdale Court, Suite 1107, Springfield, VA 22150, 703/922-7671. This support center supplies materials for military single parents.

Mothers Without Custody, P.O. Box 56762, Houston, TX 77256, 713/840-1622. This group offers legal help and mutual support and information referral service.

National Association for the Education of Young Children, 1834 Connecticut Ave., NW, Washington, DC 20009, 202/232-8777. This educational association is devoted to the education of children to age eight and provides free brochures on childcare and a bimonthly magazine.

National Center for Missing and Exploited Children, 1835 K St., NW, Suite 700, Washington, DC 20006, 202/634-9821 or 800/843-5678. Call to receive a variety of materials on abducted children.

National Committee for Citizens in Education, 410 Wilde Lake Green, Columbia, MD 21044, 301/596-5300 or 800/638-9675. This committee is concerned with educational facilities, with a special interest in programs for single parents and their children.

National Committee for Prevention of Child Abuse, 332 S. Michigan Ave., Suite 950, Chicago, IL 60604, 312/663-3520. This national organization, a resource for information and referral, is devoted to the prevention of child abuse.

National Directory of Hotlines, Evaluation Resource Association, Route 1, Box 2036, Mullica Hill, NJ 08062, 609/478-4746.

National Institute of Mental Health, 5600 Fisher Lane, Rockville, MD 20857, 703/684-7722.

National Network of Runaway and Youth Services, 905 6th St., SW, Suite 612, Washington, DC 20006, 202/488-0739.

National Runaway Switchboard, 800/421-0353 and 800/972-6006 (Illinois). This national hotline helps runaway children and their parents.

National Women's Law Center, 1751 N. St., NW, Washington, DC 20036, 202/872-0670.

Office for Child Support Enforcement and Reference Center, 6110 Executive Blvd, Rockville, MD 20852, 301/443-4442 or 443-5106 (Reference Center).

Parenting Effectiveness Training, Inc., 531 Stevens Ave., Solana Beach, CA 92075, 619/481-8121. This group conducts parenting skill groups around the country.

Parents Anonymous, 6733 S. Sepulveda, Los Angeles, CA 90046, 800/352-0386 (California), 800/421-0353 (national), and 213/371-3501 (local). This is the largest national organization devoted to preventing child abuse.

Parent Teachers Association, 700 N. Rush St., Chicago, IL 60611, 312/787-0977. A resource for educational materials, advocacy, a magazine, and legislative newsletters.

Parents Without Partners, 8807 Colesville Rd., Silver Spring, MD, 20910, 301/588-9354. This organization is the largest devoted to the welfare and interests of single parents and their children. The group publishes *The Single Parent* magazine and other resource materials.

Salvation Army, 79 Bloomfield, Verona, NJ 07044, 201/239-0606, or your local chapter. The Salvation Army provides services such as temporary foster care for children, prenatal and postnatal counseling for single mothers, family camps, and youth activities.

Single Parent Resource Center, 1165 Broadway, Suite 504, New York, NY 10001, 212/213-0047.

Step-Family Association, 28 Allegheny Ave., Suite 1307, Towson, MD 21204, 301/823-7570. The association provides information, support, and education for stepfamilies.

Tough Love, P.O. Box 1069, Doylestown, PA 18901, 215/348-7090. Tough Love is a system of self-help programs for parents and communities troubled by teen behavior nationwide and in Canada.

Widowed Persons Service, American Association of Retired Persons, 1909 K St., NW, Washington, DC 20049, 202/872-4700.

Women's Legal Defense Fund, Child Custody Project, Suite 400, 2000 P St., NW, Washington, DC 20036, 202/887-0364.

YMCA National Headquarters, 101 N. Wacker Drive, Chicago, IL 60606, 312/977-0031. The YMCA has a series of model programs sensitive to the needs of single-parent families.

Recommended Reading

Alexander, Ann. *To Live a Lie.* New York: Atheneum, 1975.

Atlas, Stephen L. *Parents without Partners.* Philadelphia: Running Press, 1984.

Authelet, Dr. Emil. *Parenting Solo.* Eugene, OR: Harvest House, 1988.

Berger, Terry. *How Does It Feel When Your Parents Get Divorced?* New York: Messner, 1976.

Bernstein, Joane E. *Books to Help Children Cope with Separation and Loss.* New York: R.R. Bowker, 1977.

Besson, Clyde C. *Picking Up the Pieces.* Milford, MI: Mott Media, Inc., 1982.

Booher, Dianna. *Coping When Your Family Falls Apart.* New York: Messner, 1979.

Brandt, Patricia and Dave Jackson. *Just Me and the Kids.* Elgin, IL: David C. Cook, 1985.

Brock, Anita. *Divorce Recovery.* Ft. Worth, TX: Worthy Publishing, 1988.

Broyard, Anatole. *Books of the Times,* Vol. II, #7.

Buchanan, Neal C. and Eugene Chamberlain. *Helping Children of Divorce.* Nashville: Broadman, 1981.

Dobson, Dr. James C. *Confident Healthy Families.* Wheaton, IL: Tyndale, 1974.

Dobson, Dr. James C. *Dare to Discipline.* Wheaton, IL: Tyndale, 1970.

Dobson, Dr. James C. *Love Must Be Tough.* Waco, TX: Word, 1983.

Dodson, Dr. Fitzhugh. *How to Single Parent.* New York: Harper & Row, 1987.

Fisher, Bruce. *Rebuilding When Your Relationship Ends.* San Luis Obispo, CA: Impact Publications, 1981.

Greywolf, Elizabeth. *The Single Mother's Handbook.* New York: Quill, 1984.

Grollman, Earl A., ed. *Explaining Divorce to Children.* Boston: Beacon Press, 1969.

Grollman, Earl A. *Talking About Divorce and Separation.* Boston: Beacon Press, 1975.

Harayda, Janice. *The Joy of Being Single.* New York: Doubleday, 1986.

Hart, Archibald D., Ph.D. *Children & Divorce: What to Expect/How to Help.* Waco, TX: Word Books, 1982.

Hensley, J. Clark. *Coping with Being Single Again.* Nashville: Broadman, 1978.

Holt, Pat and Dave, and Sandy Rau. *How Not to Raise a Cain.* Wheaton, IL: Victor Books, 1978.

Hoystead, Wesley. *You Can't Begin Too Soon.* Glendale, CA: Regal Books, 1974.

Hunt, Gary and Angela. *Mom and Dad Don't Live Together Anymore.* Eugene, OR: Harvest House, 1988.

Kehle, Dr. Mary. *In the Middle: What to do when your parents divorce.* Wheaton, IL: Shaw Publishers, 1987.

Kersey, Katherine. *Helping Your Child Handle Stress.* Washington, DC: Acropolis Press, 1986.

Krementz, Jill. *How It Feels When Parents Divorce.* New York: Alfred A. Knopf, 1988.

LeShan, Eda. *What's Going to Happen to Me?* New York: Four Winds Press, 1978.

List, Julie. *The Day the Loving Stopped: A Daughter's View of Her Parents' Divorce*. New York: Seaview Books, 1980.

Nason, Diane. *The Celebration Family.* Nashville: Thomas Nelson, 1983.

Newfield, Marcia. *A Book for Jordan*. New York: Atheneum, 1975.

Owen, Pat Hershey. *The Idea Book for Mothers*. Wheaton, IL: Tyndale, 1987.

Park, B. *Don't Make Me Smile*. New York: Alfred A. Knopf, 1981.

Pearson, Bud and Kathy. *Single Again: Remarrying for the Right Reasons*. Ventura, CA: Regal Books, 1985.

Phillips, C. *Our Family Got a Divorce*. Glendale, CA: Regal Books, 1979.

Reed, Bobbi. *I Didn't Plan to Be a Single Parent*. St. Louis: Concordia, 1981.

Robertson, John and Betty Utterback. *Suddenly Single*. New York: Simon and Schuster, 1986.

Rofes, Eric. *The Kid's Book of Divorce*. Lexington, MA: Lewis Publishing Company, 1981.

Sanderson, Jim. *How to Raise Your Kids to Stand on Their Own Two Feet*. New York: Congdon and Weed, 1983.

Sedgwick, Carolyn. *When Mothers Must Work...* Springdale, PA: Whitaker House, 1988.

Smith, B. J. *Divorced*. Wheaton, IL: Tyndale, 1983.

Smith, Harold Ivan. *Singles Ask*. Minneapolis: Augsburg, 1988.

Smith, Virginia Watts. *The Single Parent*. Old Tappan, NJ: Revell, 1976.

Streeter, Carole Sanderson. *Finding Your Place After Divorce*. Grand Rapids, MI: Zondervan, 1986.

Strom, Kay Marshall. *Chosen Families*. Grand Rapids, MI: Zondervan, 1985.

Swihart, Judson J. and Steven L. Brigham. *Helping Children of Divorce.* Downers Grove, IL: InterVarsity Press, 1982.

Swindoll, Charles R. *You and Your Child.* Nashville: Thomas Nelson, 1977.

Tayber, Edward. *Helping Your Children With Divorce.* New York: Pocket Books, 1985.

Winn, Marie. *Children Without Childhood.* New York: Pantheon Books, 1983.